THREE WOMAN – THREE STORIES

FICTION

By Teixeira Moita

1.

REMISSION

The room was cloaked in a soft, amber glow from a standing lamp, casting warm shadows on the walls. Denise sat at her desk; the cool metal of a soda can pressed against her lips. She set the can down, her movements deliberate as she retrieved her laptop bag, placed the device on the desk, and opened it. The screen flickered to life, reflecting her face in the dim light.

Denise's eyes were tired but determined, a silent testament to the battles she had been fighting. She stared at the screen, waiting. The hum of the computer filled the silence, blending with the faint background music. Her face filled the screen, as if she were live on a social media platform. Likes and emojis began to pop up around her image, a digital applause for her courage.

Without hesitation, Denise reached for a hair-cutting machine. The buzz of the clippers cut through the quiet, and she began to shave her hair to the scalp. As each lock fell, the likes and emojis multiplied, a silent, supportive roar from her online community.

Finally, she was completely bald. She took a deep breath, her reflection now a stark, powerful image of raw truth and vulnerability. She leaned into the camera.

"Yes, friends," she began, her voice steady. "I have that disease, the one no one will name. Neither the doctors nor the hospital staff will say it outright. But I will. I have cancer, and I am going to beat it."

She typed the words into the computer: "I HAVE CANCER AND I WILL BEAT IT." They appeared as a bold caption on the screen. Her cell phone buzzed with incoming messages, each one a testament to the support and love surrounding her.

"Keep your hope alive," she read aloud from a message. "Believe in the power of healing and in your ability to overcome this challenge. Remember, you are not alone. Your strength and struggle inspire those around you. That's the aim of this direct, friends. It's going to be a road full of ups and downs. Don't feel sorry for me; God is testing me and I'll get through it."

The messages continued to flood in, each one a lifeline, a beacon of hope in the vast sea of her struggle:

"I can't believe it! How can that be? Get well. A million kisses."

"Mate... how are you feeling? It's a real bummer what happened to you. We're here to support you. Strength and courage!"

"I'm not even myself... So young and beautiful. How cruel! Are you already in treatment?"

"Pray to God to heal you. He'll hear you and you'll get rid of this disease! Get well."

Denise put down her cell phone, overwhelmed by the outpouring of support. She closed her laptop, took another drink from the can, and prepared for bed. Just as she settled in, her phone rang. She answered, a familiar voice on the other end.

"Hello, darling? But what happened? I'm heartbroken!"

"What can you do?" Denise replied into the phone. "I've been caught. I've already started the treatments."

"Are you having chemotherapy?" the voice asked, filled with concern.

"Yes," Denise confirmed.

"Never underestimate the power of your determination. You are a warrior and your determination is a source of inspiration to everyone around you. I already know you... I know you'll make it. Do you need anything?"

"Nothing. I'll manage."

"Okay. If you need anything, don't hesitate. Big kiss."

"Thanks for calling. Love to you."

She hung up, but the phone rang again almost immediately. Denise sighed and answered.

"Yes?"

"Hello, darling! Joana called to tell me the sad news. I went to your page and was shocked... how are you?"

"More or less," Denise replied.

"Get well, woman! You're sorely missed. Never give up, you'll beat the disease. My uncle John has been through it and he made it. Medicine is very advanced these days. You'll see that everything will be fine."

"I have good days and bad days..." Denise started to say, but the caller interrupted.

"Bollocks! I've got to go: those damn kids knocked my TV over! Damn them! WAIT HERE, I'LL TELL YOU. I'll call you back. Love, darling."

"Kiss," Denise said, and the call ended.

A few moments passed, and the phone rang yet again. Denise answered with a weary "Yes?"

"Hi! They sent me a message saying you were ill. What's wrong, niece?"

"I have cancer."

"Damn, girl! But cancer where?"

"In the chest."

"I'll be damned! That's bad! You're being treated well, is that contagious?"

"No, Uncle... it's not contagious. I'm being followed in hospital."

"And do you do that thing that makes your hair fall out?"

"Yes, but I shaved it before it fell."

"Have you shaved your hair? Why on earth would you do that?"

"I couldn't bear to see it fall little by little."

"Damn! A girl with no hair?! That's a terrible thing! Take it easy and don't let it get you down. Well... your aunt sends you a kiss and hopes you get well soon."

"A kiss for Auntie," Denise said.

"You too. Get well. Goodbye."

The next morning, Denise awoke to the first light of dawn filtering through her curtains. She got ready for the day, her movements mechanical, as if each action took all the energy she could muster. Dressed and prepared, she left the house and took the subway, the hum of the city a backdrop to her thoughts.

She exited the metro and walked a few meters to the hospital. The imposing building loomed ahead, a place of both dread and hope. Denise took a photo of the hospital with her cell phone, a silent document of her journey, and stepped inside.

The waiting room was nearly full, a high-angle view capturing the sea of faces, each one with their own story, their own battles. Denise sat next to a fellow patient, offering a small, brave smile.

"Good morning," she greeted softly.

"Good morning," the patient replied, their voice tinged with fatigue.

"How do you feel today? Has it been difficult?" Denise asked, her voice filled with genuine concern.

"Some days worse; others better," the patient replied.

"How long have you been doing chemo?"

"I only had one treatment, about three weeks ago. Now I'm going to the doctor to have it checked out."

"It's like me: I've done the first one and I'm going to see if I can see any progress," Denise shared, feeling a kinship with this stranger.

"My dear! We still have a long way to go... we're still at the beginning."

"I have breast cancer," Denise admitted.

"Like me," the patient said softly. "How did you find out?"

"By palpation. I felt a lump in my breast and rushed to the doctor. The doctor was very attentive and immediately sent me for all the tests and... here we are. Of course, the fact that my mother had died of this disease made me more alert. Attacking the bug early on is half the cure. So, they say. And you?"

"It was a routine mammogram. I almost fainted when the doctor told me the news."

"I reacted very badly. I just cried. My husband and family were very supportive, fortunately."

"I live alone... it's difficult," Denise admitted, her voice wavering.

"No family?" the patient asked, surprised.

"Almost everyone has emigrated. I have my friends, of course, and I get a lot of support on social media."

"I don't like websites at all! Far out! It's all vanity and hypocrisy!"

"It's like everything: there are good people and not-so-good people..."

"Count me out!" the patient said firmly.

They sat in silence for a moment, the bustling waiting room around them a stark contrast to their inner turmoil. The staff continued to call out names, each one a step closer to a possible reprieve.

"Are you from around town?" Denise asked, breaking the silence.

"I come from the outskirts. It takes me almost an hour by public transport to get here."

"Fortunately, I don't live far away. For you, in addition to the illness, there's this tiredness."

"I don't even know how I've coped, or where I've found the strength for all this."

"We have to be brave," Denise said, her voice filled with quiet determination.

"What a remedy! What's more, my daughter used to bring me here, but she's in bed with the flu... COVID, or whatever it is. I've got another son, but he's a junkie; he's no good, he's out of luck!"

"I'm alone. I only have support from my friends. Only in misfortune do we see who's who."

"That's very true!" the patient agreed.

The waiting room gradually emptied. Denise watched as the patients were called, one by one, each step a reminder of the long journey ahead. Finally, the room was nearly empty, and Denise's name was not called.

She approached the counter, her heart pounding.

"Have you been seen by a doctor?" the staff member asked.

"I had an appointment..." Denise began, her voice uncertain.

"What's your name?"

"Denise."

The staff member searched the computer, frowning. "Denise? I don't have anything marked with that name..."

"My doctor booked it after the chemo session."

"How long ago was the session?"

"About three weeks..."

The staff member continued to search. "I don't have anything here. You need to contact your doctor."

"Blimey! I've come all this way..." Denise said, frustration and fatigue coloring her voice.

"I understand that. But we don't have any records."

"Well... I'm going back there. Good morning and thank you."

Denise turned to leave; her steps heavy with disappointment. The road ahead was long and uncertain, but she would face it with the same quiet strength that Denise left the hospital, the weight of the day pressing on her shoulders. She made her way home through the bustling streets, the city's noise a distant hum against her thoughts.

Her apartment welcomed her with the familiar scent of lavender and a comforting sense of solitude. She set her bag down and walked into the kitchen, preparing lunch with the ease of routine. An omelet sizzled in the pan, the aroma filling the small space.

Before her meal was ready, Denise opened her laptop and navigated to her social media page. The screen lit up with notifications: 1524 likes and dozens of comments. She scrolled through the messages, each one a tiny spark of hope in the darkness of her struggle.

"Lunch," she murmured to herself, setting the table. As she finished eating, the doorbell rang. Denise opened the door to find her friend Maria standing there, her eyes filled with concern.

Maria enveloped her in a long hug. "My dear... my dear. Why did you hide your illness from everyone? I only found out from your website."

Denise sighed, stepping back to let Maria in. "Dear Maria, I didn't want you to feel sorry for me. I preferred to suffer alone, but it was very difficult."

Maria shook her head, her grip firm on Denise's shoulders. "It's not done! Friends are for better or for worse! How do you feel?"

"Not very well. Nausea and vomiting, and extreme fatigue. The other day, after the session, I spent two days in bed."

"Have you been eating?" Maria asked, her voice laced with worry.

"I haven't had much of an appetite," Denise admitted.

"You've got to eat, girl!"

Denise managed a weak smile. "Look, I've just had lunch. I've just come back from the hospital and made an omelet."

"You don't take medication for nausea? I know what that's like from when I was pregnant..."

"I went to the hospital today for an assessment and could have ordered medication, but they didn't enter my appointment in the system... I came away empty-handed."

"It's always the same bunch of incompetents! Didn't you order with them? Bastards!"

"Maria... I was so tired of being there... I almost fell over. I'll have to see my doctor again to see what happened."

"Who is your doctor?"

Denise hesitated. "She's a new doctor. You don't know her..."

"It's not enough that you're ill, but there's also the bureaucracy getting in the way! But, Denise, be honest with me: are you being treated well?"

"I'm being monitored at the hospital. Apart from the consultation mishap, I have no complaints."

Maria frowned. "Ideally, you should be monitored and treated in a private hospital."

"Oh, Maria... you know I can't afford that!"

The doorbell rang again. Denise opened it to find her friend Ana standing there.

"Ana, what a surprise!" They greet one another with two kisses. "Hello, friend! How are you? I came as soon as I heard! It's hard to believe your bad luck!"

"What can you do?" Denise shrugged.

Ana kissed Maria on the cheek. "We were talking about treatment in a private hospital."

"That's expensive," Ana said. "And they're not always better than the others."

"But I'm being treated well," Denise insisted.

Maria turned to Ana. "Imagine, Ana... she had an appointment today. She got there, and there was nothing in the system! She left without an appointment."

"Are you serious? This country sucks!" Ana turned to Denise. "And what are you going to do?"

"I have to make an appointment with my doctor to reschedule at the hospital."

Denise got up and headed to the kitchen. "I'm going to make some tea. Anyone?"

Ana followed her. "Never mind, Denise; I'll do it. Don't get tired." She went into the kitchen.

Maria looked at Denise, her eyes filled with concern. "Have you had anyone's support? Your family? It's important not to get stuck in a hole—metaphorically speaking. Don't lose contact with people, because emotional stability is very important for healing. I know your parents are far away in Porto, but it will be important for them to visit you and support you."

"Don't worry, I'm not going to isolate myself. My uncle called me yesterday... my parents haven't called yet. I have the support of the two of you—who are my core—and I've received a surprising outpouring of support online."

"That's it! We could make our own Denise support page!"

Ana entered with a tray of tea. "I've already got the tea... I don't know where the cookies are."

"I've got them in the cupboard. I'll get them." Denise went to the kitchen.

Ana poured the tea as Denise returned with a packet of cookies. "You know what I thought?" Maria said to Ana.

"Yes?"

"Let's create a website in support of Denise."

"Great idea!" Ana agreed. "I know that these pages create a wave of solidarity and sometimes you even get some nice surprises."

Denise looked skeptical. "What? More likes?"

"Not only that: there are people who help with donations of medicine and even money!"

Denise shook her head. "I'm not really into public solicitation. And I don't want my name on everyone's lips; I like my privacy. Besides, I don't have the strength to run a website."

"Don't worry," Maria reassured her. "We'll take care of everything, right Ana?"

"Of course! Count me in! With luck, we'll even be able to raise money for your treatment. There are websites where we can create a project to ask for financial help for Denise to be treated in private hospitals! Contrary to popular belief, there are very supportive people who are making your fight their own. Believe me!"

"That's great, Ana!" Maria said. "It's called crowdfunding. I know of a case where someone picked up a dog that had been hit by a car on the road and raised money for its treatment... the dog had already been operated on and they were still collecting donations on the website."

Ana searched on her mobile. "I think I know a website... here it says, for example: *'This site is amazing! I raised about 10,000 EUROS in less than 48 hours for my nephew's medical needs.'*

"48 hours? Hard to believe."

Ana turned to Denise. "You don't trust the human race..."

"And why should I start trusting? The human race is a disordered mixture of selfishness, greed, and ignorance wrapped up in civilization. I have no disappointments because I have no illusions about the human race. I don't remember who wrote this..."

"I think it was Saramago," Maria said.

"Another skeptic. Soon we'll be talking about Nietzsche! The human race has everything you say, it's true. But we also have altruism, the hero... Human nature is often paradoxical, with people displaying a wide range of behaviors and characteristics. We can be both generous and selfish, brave and cowardly, loving and cruel—all at the same time."

"Well, let's stop being skeptical," Maria said, turning to Denise. "Try public hospitals to find out how much treatment costs. Just give them a call; you don't have to get tired anymore and we'll take care of the page. Okay?"

"Okay, friends. Thanks for everything."

They had tea and cookies, the conversation lightening the heavy mood. Denise offered, "Do you like these gingerbread cookies? Maybe they're a bit hard. They're made by a neighbor."

Ana laughed. "My neighbors give me nothing! All I get is noise, TVs blaring, kids playing ball in the house, and moaning late at night."

"Now I'm the one who's looking good for a fiancé!" Denise joked.

"Don't be silly, Denise! Is that something to say? You always look beautiful! Just because you look hairless doesn't mean you've lost all your beauty," Maria said.

"Beauty is on the inside. Rubbish!"

"Maria's right," Ana agreed. "How many women are eighty years old and still look beautiful underneath the wrinkles and so on?"

"Yeah... you're right. I'm a bit discouraged at not having had the appointment..."

"We'll sort it out. We'll be lucky, you'll see. You'll have enough money to be treated in a decent hospital and you won't have these situations anymore. Let's believe it!"

"That's right! You'll be as good as new, don't worry," Maria added.

"Tonight, I'll deal with the crowdfunding page. Let's talk," Ana said as they prepared to leave.

After they left, Denise tidied up the kitchen and lay down on the sofa, turning on the TV. The familiar sounds of a sitcom filled the room as she drifted into a restless sleep.

Denise was having dinner when her cell phone rang. She answered, "Yes? Ana?"

"Good evening, Denise. I'm calling because I've got a friend who's working on your crowdfunding page. She's an ace at IT!"

"Good! I'm glad. Who is this friend?"

"Gloria. You know her... she runs that association against domestic violence."

"A redhead we met at that demonstration in September?"

"That's the one! She's very willing. I told her about you and the idea we had, and she volunteered straight away! Gloria is very comfortable on social media and does online campaigns with the greatest of ease."

"Good news! Only good news!"

"It is, isn't it? Now, she's going to need some things from you."

"What do you mean?"

"Things to put on the page. Photos of you, before and after your hair fell out; and, to give it more credibility, a certificate from the hospital, showing you're undergoing treatment. People don't know you and might think it's all a hoax. She says you can get the certificate online, just go to the Social Security website. And send her your bank details too!"

"Okay. No problem, I'll take care of it."

"Excellent! I'll send you her email by SMS. As soon as possible, you can send me the photos and the certificate. Big kiss!"

Denise hung up the phone, feeling a mix of hope and apprehension. She spent a few moments in the bathroom, collecting herself. Returning to the living room, she straightened the cushions and sat down at her desk. She opened her laptop; the familiar Windows start-up sound a small comfort in the quiet room.

For the next hour, Denise worked on gathering the necessary documents. She scanned her hospital certificate, which read:

"I HEREBY CERTIFY THAT DENISE MENDES IS UNDERGOING TREATMENT AT THIS HOSPITAL FOR: BREAST CANCER - STAGE 2. THE DIRECTION."

With a deep breath, Denise sent the documents to Gloria, hoping this small act of trust would bring some relief to her weary heart.

***

A week had passed since Denise decided to embrace her new reality. The world outside her apartment seemed both familiar and alien, as if she was seeing it through different eyes. She stepped out, the fabric of her headscarf fluttering slightly in the gentle morning breeze. It had become her constant companion, a symbol of her journey, a shield against curious eyes.

As she drove to the supermarket, Denise felt a sense of normalcy in the mundane act of parking and grabbing a shopping trolley. The aisles were a maze of colors and choices, each turn revealing more possibilities. She moved with purpose, but also with an air of distraction, lost in her thoughts until a voice broke through her reverie.

"Excuse me… you look like… I'm sure… you're not Denise?"

The customer's inquiry was tentative but hopeful.

Denise's heart skipped a beat. "Yes, I am," she admitted, her voice barely above a whisper.

"I thought so! We're internet friends! I follow your page and I'm a fan," the customer gushed, her eyes shining with recognition.

"Fan!" Denise echoed; the word foreign on her lips. "O… o… thank you. But there's nothing to admire about me."

"So modest! Of course there is! Your courage and determination are an encouragement and an example to all of us - women!" The customer's admiration was palpable.

Denise offered a small smile, touched by the kindness. "So, I'm glad. Thank you."

The customer launched into her story without pause, sharing her own grief and admiration for Denise's strength. Denise listened, her heart going out to the woman who had faced so much yet found solace in Denise's journey.

As the customer finally departed with well-wishes, Denise continued her shopping with a heavier heart but also with a renewed sense of purpose.

Denise completes her shopping and makes her way to the cashier. After settling the bill with her credit card, she moves towards the exit. A subtle instinct draws her to the ATM. As she withdraws cash and retrieves the receipt, a sudden whirlwind of surprise engulfs her, causing her to momentarily lose her footing and sense of reality.

After settled in her car, Denise dialed Ana's number with trembling fingers. The supermarket encounter had left her shaken, but it was the ATM receipt that truly rocked her world.

"Denise? Hello, my dear!" Ana's voice was warm over the phone.

"Hi, Ana, what's up?" Denise tried to sound casual despite the whirlwind of emotions.

"Yes, fine. How have you been?" Ana's concern was evident.

"I was shopping in the supermarket and checked the balance in my bank account…" Denise trailed off, still in disbelief.

"Isn't it fantastic! Gloria has done a wonderful job of spreading the word on the Internet. People are joining in and supporting it wonderfully," Ana enthused.

"But, Ana… I have more than three thousand in my bank balance! In one week!" Denise's voice was a mix of shock and awe.

"Yes, I saw it yesterday! Your beautiful, powerful and emotional posts have had a huge impact! We're a success story! And the subscribers to your page? Over a hundred thousand! Have you seen this?" Ana's excitement bubbled through the phone.

"I'm dizzy… this is overwhelming. But who are all these people, Ana?" Denise asked, trying to grasp the magnitude of their support.

"Don't worry, Denise. Get your treatments and don't worry about the rest… Contrary to popular belief, people have hearts - it's not just selfishness these days," Ana reassured her.

"But this is stratospheric! How did your friend Gloria do it?" Denise wondered aloud.

"It wasn't her or me: it was YOU! It was your beautiful soul that moved the world. You just have to keep being yourself," Ana said with conviction.

. "It was your beautiful soul that moved the world. You just have to keep being yourself. Don't be impressed by the numbers, otherwise you'll lose the naturalness that is your trademark."

Ana always knew the right words to say. Her voice, even in absence, felt like a warm embrace. Denise could almost see her, her friend's earnest eyes urging her to focus on the good, on the people she was helping.

"You're helping them too," Ana had said. "These people feel better about themselves for helping… it brings them comfort and they have the same goal in life as you: healing!"

"But… it's an audience and I have to keep that audience!" Denise had voiced her fear aloud during one of their conversations.

"Denise… focus on your healing and keep doing what you've been doing so far. That's the secret to your success: see people as friends - which is what they are."

"I'm starting to get scared," Denise had admitted, her voice barely above a whisper.

"Why be afraid? You have thousands of people who support and love you! Consider it a very good thing that will get you through your illness."

Denise opened her eyes and stared at the car ceiling. Ana was right. She just had to be herself, to show her gratitude and share her journey honestly. "You may be right," she whispered to the empty room. "I just have to feel grateful and respond accordingly, don't I?"

"That's right!" Ana's voice came again, clear and encouraging. "When you post on your page, it means you're alive and fighting. It brightens their day. A donation, in this case, is an act of love, not pity. You are family to these subscribers. Denise, darling: draw strength from that love they're giving you and choose the best hospitals - no worries - because more money is still coming in and you can choose the best of the best."

Denise smiled, a small but genuine smile. "You're right, as always, Ana."

Denise remembered the conversation clearly as she returns to the supermarket. She picked up a cart and started her shopping again, the mundane task a welcome distraction from her racing thoughts. As she filled her cart, she found herself in front of the liquor section:

"What is the best whiskey?" she asked the store employee, her voice firm despite her inner turmoil.

The employee looked at the display case, opened a glass door, and took out a bottle. "This is very good…"

"But… which is the most expensive?"

The employee hesitated, then put the bottle back and picked up another. "We have this one…, but it costs two hundred and fifty."

"I'll take that one.", Denise takes the bottle that the waiter brings to her and puts it in her shopping cart. Denise returns home. The whirlwind of feelings and anguish has made her drive all the way almost by instinct.

Denise paid and headed to her car, the weight of her purchase matching the heaviness in her heart. She drove home in silence, the whiskey - a strange comfort in the passenger seat. As she unloaded her groceries, her mind wandered to the upcoming interview. Ana had called her yesterday with the news.

***

Now, at home, she consults her notebook and is amazed once again at the scale of it all.

Denise turned off her laptop and leaned back in her chair, closing her eyes. She was tired, so very tired. The survival, the fatigue, the constant battle—it all seemed endless. But Ana's words reminded her why she kept going.

As if they were in a connection of thoughts, Ana calls, now to indicate that there is a television channel that wants to interview her.

"A television channel? But, Ana, I don't know if I can…" Denise had protested.

"Yes, you can. The thing is, our campaign is a success and they want to interview you. It's a quick thing… is that OK?"

"All right, let them come." She reluctantly acquiesced as yet another burden they were placing on his shoulders

***

The next day came quickly. Denise went about her daily routine, trying to ignore the gnawing anxiety in her gut. She had lunch, read a book, watched TV, and spent some time on her laptop. When the doorbell finally rang, she took a deep breath and opened the door.

"Hello, good afternoon!" she greeted Julia, Ana, and the TV crew.

"Hello, baby!" Ana kissed her on the cheek. "This is Julia, from Channel 5."

"At last, we meet the heroine!" Julia hugged Denise tightly. "Ready to become a universal icon? It's a short report, but I guarantee it will have an impact on the country! In my career, I've interviewed many personalities, but Denise is something special: what courage, what knowledge!"

They settled in the living room, Julia giving instructions to the cameraman while Denise tried to calm her racing heart. She had never been comfortable in the spotlight, but this was important. People needed to hear her story.

"Good afternoon, viewers, we're here to interview Denise. Denise is a heroine and an example to all women," Julia began, her tone professional but warm. She turned to Denise. "Denise, we know you have cancer… how did that happen?"

Denise looks at Julia, with astonishment and a little contempt.

"Good afternoon and thank you, Julia. I don't know how it happened. All I know is that a few months ago I had a routine mammogram and it showed a cancerous lump in my breast."

"A cancerous lump in the breast: that's how it all begins. How did you feel when you found out?"

Denise's mind flashed back to that moment, the crushing weight of the diagnosis. "I felt sick, of course. I cried a lot and didn't eat anything for almost three days."

"Now… that was a diet!" Julia quipped, but Denise could only manage a weak smile in response.

"How long did it take you to find out since you took the test?" Julia pressed on.

"Six months."

"Six months? That long? How is that possible? Health in this country is going from bad to worse!" Julia turned to the camera, launching into a brief tirade about the state of the healthcare system.

Denise took a deep breath, gathering her strength. "Well… I've been using alternative medicine and I've been feeling better."

"Alternative medicine? What do you mean?"

"I'm being treated by a specialist from China. Medicine there is very advanced. The advantage is that the treatments don't harm the patient's health so much."

Julia looked skeptical. "Chinese medicine is a bit… different. It's a controversial issue. Some people think it's fraudulent and sometimes expensive."

"The donations, for which I am very grateful, have been a fantastic help. As for alternative medicines, they've been around for thousands of years and have the advantage of minimal side effects."

Julia nodded, though Denise could see the doubt in her eyes. "How do you see the future?"

"I don't think about the future," Denise admitted. "I try to live each day - not as if it were my last, but as if it were just another day."

***

The interview ended, and the TV crew left. Denise felt a strange emptiness as she watched them go. She lay down on her bed, exhaustion washing over her. Ana's words from their earlier conversation echoed in her mind.

"Denise… focus on your healing and keep doing what you've been doing so far."

She drifted into a restless sleep, waking hours later to the sound of her phone ringing. It was Maria.

"I've just seen the interview on Seven O'clock News, and you were wonderful! The interview is already being quoted everywhere! YOU ARE A STAR!"

"That's what I didn't want…" Denise muttered, a feeling of dread creeping in.

"Everyone dreams of it! And you'll be able to triple the donations on your site, so you can get the treatments!"

"I think I've got enough there."

"Are you depressed?" Maria's voice was full of concern.

"All this attention… the fame… it confuses me."

"Enjoy the limelight for as long as you have left."

"How much time do I have left? What do you mean?"

"I didn't express myself well… I meant: make the most of the free time you have…"

Denise hung up, her mind swirling with conflicting emotions.

***

The next day, Denise was cutting her toenails when a loud knock interrupted her thoughts. She put on her robe and opened the door, only to be met by a barrage of reporters and cameras.

"What do you have to say about the allegations of fraud?"

"Do you confess to being a dishonest person who wanted to take advantage of people's kindness?"

"Are you going to give the money back, or have you already spent it all?"

Denise slammed the door shut, her heart pounding. She threw herself onto the sofa, tears streaming down her face. The doorbell rang again, insistently.

One can hear, from outside the door: "DENISE! IT'S ANA! OPEN UP, PLEASE!"

She hesitated, wiping her tears, and slowly opened the door. Ana rushed in; her face full of concern.

"Denise, what's happening? What's all this about fraud?"

Denise collapsed into Ana's arms, sobbing uncontrollably. "I don't know, Ana. I don't know…"

Ana held her tightly, whispering words of comfort. "We'll get through this, Denise. I promise. We'll get through this together."

And in that moment, amidst the chaos and accusations, Denise found a small glimmer of hope in her friend's unwavering support.

Denise woke up to a dull ache in her chest, not from any physical pain, but from the weight of a thousand eyes bearing down on her. She looked at herself in the mirror in the living room, her face pale and drawn, eyes hollowed by sleepless nights. The lines around her mouth had deepened, etching a permanent mark of anxiety. She sighed and turned away from the reflection, a figure she barely recognized anymore.

Her phone buzzed incessantly on the nightstand, the screen lighting up with messages and missed calls. Ignoring it, she pulled herself out of bed and padded to the living room, followed by Ana, where the remnants of last night's whiskey still sat on the coffee table. She poured herself a small glass and took a sip, hoping it would steady her nerves.

As she sat on the couch, the doorbell rang. Denise hesitated, then forced herself to get up and answer it. Ana stepped inside - Her face a mask of concern. The sound of shouting from outside filtered through the door as Ana closed behind

"What's that out there?" Denise asked, her voice barely above a whisper.

"It's the press," Ana replied, closing the door behind her. "They want answers."

"Why? What do they want from me?"

Ana took a deep breath, her eyes scanning Denise's face for any sign of comprehension. "Remember that hospital document we put on the website? The one with the QR code?"

Denise nodded; her mind foggy.

"Someone scanned it with their phone. The document belonged to someone else. It was for Dengue treatment, not cancer."

Denise stared at Ana, the weight of her words slowly sinking in. "Now everyone wants my head," she murmured.

"Denise, do you have cancer?" Ana asked, her voice trembling.

After a long pause, Denise shook her head. "No. I've never had cancer."

Ana's eyes widened in shock. "My God, Denise... why? What were you thinking?"

"I don't know," Denise replied, her voice breaking. "I had nothing in life. No one cared about me. I thought... I thought if I did this, people would notice me. I wanted to be someone."

Ana sat down heavily on the couch. "How can you be someone with this farce? Hundreds of people gave their money."

Denise jumps "I have nothing to do with donations. People donate to clean up their sins! They're mean to their parents; they're mean to their spouses; they're mean to their co-workers; they're mean to their neighbors; they're mean to other people!

They're not even remorseful: they just want to clean up their sins! Do they repent? No! They give money to buy dry cleaning for the shit they do every day! Then they come across a poor girl with cancer, who doesn't bother them, and they are filled with compassion to feel that they have something inside those empty souls. Don't feel sorry for them at all, Ana! Contrary to what you think, they don't care about me at all. I'm just another instrument to fill their illusion that they're people! These people are so small, petty, mediocre, who need a cancerous woman to make them somebody, and all it takes is for his name to appear on the website saying that Mr.-Son-of- a-very-large-bitch donated two hundred for everyone to see how pious, generous and unselfish he is! And he gets to see his name and look at the donation, feeling like the hero of the destitute ladies of the Middle Ages!

Things have taken on proportions that none of us imagined. You can see the number of idiots who want to purge the shriveled soul hanging from their skeletons.

Did I feel good about all this? Good and bad. Good, because - finally - someone was paying attention to me. On the other hand, I felt bad for you, for Maria, for Gloria…

Nothing is perfect. Even the scam isn't perfect.

Denise's eyes hardened. "That was your and Maria's idea, not mine. People donate to ease their own guilt. They're not remorseful; they just want to clean their consciences. They don't care about me at all. I'm just a tool for them to feel better about themselves."

Ana shook her head in disbelief. "What about the money, Denise?"

Denise stood up and walked to the kitchen, returning with an almost empty bottle of whiskey. "I spent it on this," she said, holding up the bottle. "I didn't buy jewelry or go to fancy restaurants. I spent it on whiskey."

Ana's face softened with pity. "Denise, you're not well."

"Now I'm not," Denise snapped. "I was fine when people cared. Now I have nothing, not even dignity."

"What are you going to do?" Ana asked.

Denise squared her shoulders, a look of determination in her eyes. "I'm going to go out there and confront them."

She stormed to her room, emerging moments later wearing an overcoat that hung awkwardly on her thin frame. Without another word, she opened the front door and stepped outside.

The reporters and photographers surged forward, their cameras flashing, voices shouting questions. Denise raised her hands for silence.

"Good afternoon," she said, her voice steady. "I want to make a statement. There are many ways to fight for a cause. Some demonstrate in the streets, others sign petitions or put pressure on politicians. I had a cause, and I chose my way of fighting. Whether you agree or disagree, the fact remains that because of me, the subject of breast cancer was talked about. This was my fight."

A reporter shouted, "And what did you do with the money?"

Denise took a deep breath. "The money will be given to hospital institutions dedicated to breast cancer research."

The crowd erupted into a frenzy. Suddenly, a man pushed through the throng, his face contorted with rage. "You're a crook and a liar! My wife died of cancer!" he screamed, pulling out a gun and firing two shots.

Denise felt a searing pain and crumpled to the ground. The world faded to black as screams and cries echoed around her.

***

One month later, Ana parked her car outside an old retirement home. The building stood solemnly amidst large gardens, its walls bearing the marks of time. She walked to the entrance and rang the doorbell.

A voice crackled over the intercom. "Yes?"

"Good afternoon. I'm here to visit Mrs. Denise Mendes," Ana replied.

The gate buzzed open, and Ana made her way through the garden. A nurse greeted her at the door. "Good afternoon. I'll bring Mrs. Denise."

Ana sat on a bench, watching as people in wheelchairs and on crutches moved slowly through the garden. After a while, Denise appeared, pushed in a wheelchair by the nurse

"How is she?" Ana asked.

"The same," the nurse replied. "She can't speak; she can't walk. The bullet hit a vital point in her brain."

The nurse left them alone. Ana sat beside Denise, taking her hand. "My dear... what have you done?" she whispered. "You played with death, that's what it was."

Denise's eyes met Ana's, a silent apology passing between them. She gently squeezed Ana's hand; the only communication left to her. They sat in silence, hands clasped together. The trees in the garden stood as silent witnesses, capturing the moment of connection and the unspoken bond that still remained.

***

2.

PREGNANCY

PREGNANCY

by

Teixeira Moita

***

Rosa sits in her car, her hand instinctively resting on her rounded belly. She absentmindedly eats a snack, her eyes occasionally flitting to her reflection in the rearview mirror as she adjusts her makeup. Her phone lies beside her, a silent witness to her anticipation. The large company building looms in the background, casting long shadows in the late afternoon sun.

After what feels like an eternity, the door to the building swings open, and Fred emerges. He walks with the assured, unhurried stride of someone who has spent years mastering the art of corporate diplomacy. His tailored suit and polished shoes exude confidence, but the sight of Rosa halts him in his tracks. He stares at her, a mix of surprise and apprehension in his eyes.

"Fred!" Rosa calls out, her voice breaking the stillness of the parking lot. She rushes towards him, the weight of her pregnancy making her steps deliberate.

Fred's face contorts in astonishment. "Rosa! What are you doing here?"

"I need to talk to you," she replies, her tone a mixture of determination and vulnerability.

Fred glances around nervously. "You shouldn't be here, Rosa. It's too risky. Someone might see us."

Rosa's gaze hardens. "What's the matter, Fred? No one ever knew about us."

Fred sighs, his eyes darting to her belly. "I'm married, Rosa. This could cause a lot of problems for me."

Rosa places a protective hand over her belly. "Well, Fred, this 'problem' is because I'm pregnant."

Fred's eyes widen. "Pregnant?"

"Yes, Fred. Pregnant. That's how babies are made. Didn't anyone ever tell you?"

Fred's face pales. "How long are you pregnant?"

Rosa's laugh is devoid of humor. "Yes, Fred. Seven months. Congratulations."

They stand there, the silence between them heavy and oppressive. Finally, Fred clears his throat. "Let's go somewhere private to talk."

***

They sit in a small cafe on the outskirts of town, the aroma of coffee mingling with the quiet hum of conversation around them. Fred orders a coffee and a donut, his attempt at normalcy falling flat. Rosa, despite his insistence on something more elaborate, settles for a simple tea.

The silence between them is thick with unspoken words. Fred finally breaks it. "So, what's been happening with you?"

Rosa stirs her tea slowly. "The usual. I'm still at the bank. And Mifa is still with me."

Fred raises an eyebrow. "The cat?"

Rosa's eyes narrow. "Yes, Fred. The cat. Why wouldn't I have her?"

Fred fidgets with his coffee cup. "I heard pets can be dangerous for newborns."

Rosa scoffs. "Fred, what century are you living in? Mifa is fine. She's not going anywhere."

Fred's shoulders slump. "I just heard things. I don't know."

Rosa leans back in her chair, her eyes never leaving Fred's face. "What about you? What's been happening in your life?"

Fred sighs. "The company is doing well. the company will now enter the stock exchange soon. But personally, things are... complicated."

Rosa's voice drips with sarcasm. "Complications with the wife?"

Fred hesitates. "Divorce isn't an option."

Rosa's laugh is bitter. "Of course, it's not. That ring on your finger isn't a symbol of love; it's a shackle."

Fred looks away, unable to meet her gaze. "I'm sorry, Rosa. I never wanted to hurt you."

Rosa's eyes fill with tears she refuses to let fall. "You did hurt me, Fred. You left without a word, without an explanation."

Fred's voice is barely a whisper. "I was lost. I still am."

***

Memories flood Rosa's mind, unbidden and painful. She recalls their arguments, the sharp words thrown like daggers, the objects shattered in fits of rage. She remembers the nights alone, the crushing weight of his absence, the hollow ache of her broken heart.

Fred's voice pulls her back to the present. "I haven't had a moment's peace in so long. My life is a constant whirlwind of meetings, deadlines, and demands. I feel like I'm drowning."

Rosa's voice is soft but firm. "And you thought our relationship was a lifeline?"

Fred's eyes fill with regret. "I don't know what I thought. I just know that I hurt you, and I'm sorry."

Rosa takes a deep breath, steadying herself. "Sorry doesn't change anything, Fred. I'm pregnant with your child, and I need to know what you're going to do about it."

Fred's face crumples. "I don't know. I can't leave my family, but I don't want to abandon you either."

Rosa's voice is cold. "You already did."

***

The cafe fades into a memory of a bookstore, where Rosa first saw Fred. She was there with her friend Martha, who had dragged her out of her apartment and into a public book presentation. The author's reading had been a blur, but Fred's presence had been electric. They had stood in line for autographs, exchanged smiles, and later, words that sparked a connection.

Rosa's mind drifts to that first conversation, the way Fred had looked at her, the way he had made her feel seen. She remembers the thrill of their early dates, the excitement of their secret meetings, the passion that had burned between them.

But now, all that remains is the reality of her pregnancy and Fred's unwillingness to step up.

***

"I could help you with some amount of money…", says Fred eagerly.

Rosa's voice cuts through the memories. "You can't just offer me money and think that solves everything, Fred"

Fred's eyes widen in surprise. "I didn't mean it like that. I just... I don't know what else to do."

Rosa's voice trembles with anger. "You could start by being there for your child. By being a father."

Fred's face crumples. "I'm trying, Rosa. I really am."

Rosa stands, her resolve hardening. "Try harder, Fred. Because I'm not doing this alone."

She wants to leave the cafe, the weight of her decision settling on her shoulders. She knows the road ahead will be difficult, but she's determined to face it head-on. For her child, for herself, and for the life she's chosen to bring into the world.

***

Her heart seems to faint heavy with the realization that she cannot rely on him. She knows she must forge her own path, one that doesn't depend on broken promises and half-hearted apologies. The future is uncertain, but Rosa faces it with a newfound strength and determination.

She dreams of walking away right now, the sound of her footsteps echoing in the quiet cafe, leaving Fred behind to grapple with the consequences of his actions.

Fred found himself lost in the reflection of his past, the worn dedication on the front page of his book a poignant reminder of the days gone by. He hadn't seen Rosa in months, and yet here she was, sitting across from him in the dimly lit café, the air thick with unsaid words and unresolved emotions.

Rosa's eyes, still sharp and inquisitive, seemed to search his soul as they had always done. He felt a familiar pang of guilt and longing. The *book* between them was more than just a collection of pages; it was a relic of their shared history, a history that Fred had meticulously avoided confronting until now.

***

Rosa relives in her mind, their first meeting at the book presentation:

Fred took a deep breath, breaking the silence that had settled between them like an uninvited guest. "I bet your dedication is better than mine," he said, his voice tinged with a mixture of nostalgia and regret.

Rosa looked up; her suspicion evident. "What?"

"I bet your dedication is better than mine…" Fred repeated, his attempt at a smile faltering under her gaze.

Rosa's brow furrowed. "I heard. But why do you say that?"

Fred sighed, the weight of his confession pressing down on him. "I know the author—he likes beautiful women."

A shadow of a smile crossed Rosa's lips. "It seems he's not the only one…"

Fred laughed, a hollow sound that echoed in the cavern of his memories. "Well answered!"

The silence stretched again, a chasm that neither seemed willing to cross. Finally, Fred spoke. "If I show you my dedication, will you show me yours?"

Rosa hesitated, her hand hovering over the book. "A dedication is a personal thing… I don't even know you!"

Fred extended his hand, a gesture of reconciliation. "Fred Jones, nice to meet you."

Rosa hesitated for a moment before taking his hand. "Rosa Williams."

Martha, who had been sitting silently, stood up and kissed Rosa on both cheeks. "As I told you, I have to go," she said abruptly, leaving without another word.

Rosa stared after Martha, stunned by her sudden departure. Fred's voice pulled her back to the present. "So, what do you say? Let's compare dedications."

Rosa glanced from Fred to the door, still processing Martha's exit. "I… don't…"

Fred pressed on. "Shall we compare dedications?"

"Comparing dedications?" Rosa repeated, her mind still elsewhere.

"Yes, we see what the author has written in each of the dedications. I'll show you my book, and Rosa, show me yours. I bet he wrote 'Beauty' on yours…" Fred's voice was a mix of challenge and hope.

Rosa finally focused on him, her eyes narrowing. "Were you born this cheeky, or are there are free online courses for cheeky people?"

Fred laughed, opening his book. "So, I read you what the author decided to write me in his dedication." He cleared his throat theatrically.

"'To Fred, with the greatest esteem, the author.' You can't say it's poetry. Besides, he's my son's teacher."

Rosa's curiosity piqued despite herself. "He may know your son, but he probably doesn't know you."

Fred nodded, conceding the point. "You may be right there. But show me your dedication; I'm curious. I have hundreds of autographed books at home. Did you know that an autographed book can be worth up to ten times as much?"

Rosa smiled, a genuine expression this time. "So… if it's a first edition with an autograph…"

Fred's eyes lit up. "Wow! Then we're already in the stratosphere!"

"So… apart from being a collector of autographed books, what is your profession? Teacher, like the author?"

Fred shook his head. "No. Far from that area. I'm CEO of a company here in town."

Rosa raised an eyebrow. "Well, if you're a CEO, you can buy all the autographed books you want…"

Fred leaned back, a wistful look in his eyes. "The problem isn't buying them; the problem is finding the time to read them. I have a very busy life, as you can probably imagine… but I recognize that one of my greatest passions is books: I really enjoy Art books, those little books with photos of paintings and sculptures, and I have quite a collection of them."

"I have some too," Rosa admitted.

Fred's face lit up with excitement. "Building a personal library is a form of expression and self-discovery. The act of collecting physical books is often driven by a passion for literature. Let's say… the aesthetics of the covers or the search for special and rare editions. Feeling the weight of the book in my hands and leafing through its pages adds a tactile dimension to the reading experience. The texture of the paper, especially in high-quality editions, can be a pleasure in and of itself. I won't say no to an old book, either. Old books carry with them the history of those who previously owned them. Notes, dedications, and even marks of use contribute to a sense of continuity and connection with past readers."

Rosa watched him, a mixture of admiration and skepticism in her eyes. "Wow! We have a refined CEO here!"

Fred chuckled. "I'd like to invite you to my library now, but… hum, I'm having some work done at home." He paused, his tone softening. "But… you still haven't shown me your dedication!"

Rosa shook her head. "Let's leave it like this in its seclusion…"

"As you wish," Fred replied, a hint of disappointment in his voice.

***

The café seemed to fade around them as they slipped into their memories.

Fred broke the silence again. "Remember when we first met? You never showed me the dedication. What was so personal about it?"

Rosa's eyes flashed with old pain. "I had to hide it from you. Furthermore, it seems you had more secrets than the planet Mars!"

Fred sighed, rubbing his temples. "You're not going to start with recriminations… You, me, and the world have changed a lot since we stopped seeing each other and terminated our relationship."

"Relationship?" Rosa's voice was sharp. "That wasn't a relationship at all! A few dinners on the sly, a few visits to my apartment, a few shags. That wasn't a relationship. Those were episodes of a cheap TV series. But you were comfortable and guarded about it; you never assumed anything. You had all the space in the world, and I only had room to wait. I wanted affection, a healthy relationship, stability, and you, always elusive, with no answers, shrugging your shoulders, leaving me with no answers. You didn't even make promises! And there I was, trapped in a gilded cage, and the only thing that didn't make me wither away were my expectations—I created and fed those expectations myself!"

Fred looked away; guilt etched in every line of his face. "We've been over this a thousand times. I was conditioned. My life is a game of Mikado: if any stick goes out-of-place everything falls apart." He paused, looking back at her. "And you… how are things at the bank?"

Rosa's expression softened, slightly. "I'm not complaining. They demand more and more from their workers and pay less. Every day, the bank increases its profits. What about your company surroundings?"

Fred shrugged. "There were no major changes. We now have a new finance director: Garcia has gone to another company. Do you remember Garcia?"

"No," Rosa replied flatly.

"I'm sure you remember him… He was the one who, at a Christmas party, got so drunk that he broke his foot dancing! And no one could lift him off the floor because he insisted; he wanted to take a nap!" Fred laughed, but the sound was hollow.

Rosa's lips twitched in a ghost of a smile. "It's always been like that, Fred."

Fred nodded. "It's always been like this, Fred."

Rosa sighed. "Respect is a very nice thing."

Fred raised an eyebrow. "You're saying it sarcastically, but that's just it. Our grandparents had that saying for a reason. They used to respect hierarchies."

"My dear… Freedom of expression at work is one of the main characteristics of organizations. It's no coincidence that this attribute appears in all surveys. Employees who speak their minds are the ones who care most about their companies. They are the ones who still want to find the right answer to problems. What I've learned from my good and bad bosses, I try to apply in my day-to-day life. Nowadays, there's no longer any room for dummies."

Fred shook his head. "Lots of small talk and living most for the intrigue than for work—that's what these rats do…"

Rosa leaned forward. "Since we are talking about work… do you remember me talking about Silva from the Audit Department at my bank?"

Fred's brow furrowed. "I think so… Yes, a creep who was always harassing you with sexual innuendos."

Rosa's eyes sparkled with a hint of mischief. "Exactly! Do you want to know what happened to him?"

"What happened to him?"

"He's dead."

Fred stared at her, stunned. "Good heavens!"

"But… listen, it's the way he died; that's a joke." Rosa's eyes twinkled with dark humor.

"How can someone's death be funny?!"

"Wait…" Rosa laughed, her voice filled with a strange glee. "A vein burst in his brain when he was straining to shit in the toilet." She burst into laughter.

Fred stared in astonishment before a stifled laugh escaped him, growing into a full belly laugh. They laughed together, the absurdity of the moment bridging the chasm between them.

"He pulled so hard…" Rosa managed between laughs.

"He wanted to save on laxatives!" Fred laughed harder.

"Poor devil," Rosa said, wiping tears of laughter from her eyes.

"What a fucking death!" Fred's laughter finally subsided, a grin lingering on his face.

***

The laughter faded, and Fred glanced at his wristwatch. "Are you in a hurry?" Rosa asked.

"I have a meeting in a little while." Fred took his cell phone out of his jacket, checking the mails.

"You never had much time for me…" Rosa's voice was soft, but the accusation was clear.

"Here we go. Do you want to talk to me or just shoot more arrows at St. Sebastian?" Fred's frustration was palpable.

"You're not much of a martyr," Rosa retorted.

Fred leaned back; his expression weary. "The fact is that I was tormented during our relationship by your demands, tantrums, and whims. Why do you think we broke up? You've created such an atmosphere between us that we've reached a breaking point."

Rosa replies, almost like a sigh "So… it was my fault."

"It was life's fault. There were too many people getting in the way. We didn't understand each other; although I understood your anguish, you didn't understand my limitations. It was always me who didn't want to… I couldn't… give you what you wanted—the life you dreamed of with me. It was my fault for knowing you and wanting you… I could turn around and run away and dream of your image in my mind forever… living in the fantasy of knowing you and wanting you… but dreams have no hands, no lips, no body… In dreams, we are alone with a fuzzy image of a person—that wasn't good enough for me: I had to get to know you, hear your voice, listen to your opinions, and learn from you, even though you were much younger than me. In short, I wanted to feel you, but—I admit—because I was married with a family, I was very confined in what I could give. It was my fault, yes. But not that negligent, willful fault. I never wanted to hurt you or make you suffer… Excuse the common phrase, but that's how I feel."

Fred paused, the weight of his words hanging in the air. "I liked the months we spent together. I liked your detachment from material things when everything around me revolved around material goods: money, cars, houses, expensive trips, restaurants, clothes… You were the opposite: you were content with little and with the beauty of the simplicity with which you lived. I loved you, longed for you, and was happy, then…"

"Then the riots started," Rosa finished for him, her voice flat.

"Riots… we can call it that."

"But… the sex was good, at least."

"At least? Don't diminish things like that."

"Hey, man… but was it good for you or not?"

***

Fred's mind drifted to the past, a vivid memory flooding back:

They were at Rosa's apartment, the air thick with anticipation. Rosa struggled to get the key to the door as Fred pinched her and bit her gently on the neck.

"Ouch! Get off me, you bastard!" Rosa laughed, trying to push him away with little conviction.

Fred kissed her neck, his voice a low growl. "Fred! I can't open the door like this!"

Finally, they stumbled inside, shedding clothes and inhibitions. Fred's words were a murmur against her skin. "You're such a fragile and desirable butterfly…"

Rosa laughed, the sound pure and carefree. "Butterfly? Corny, but I like it. Flying from flower to flower—I like that."

Fred stopped; his expression serious. "Did you want to fly from flower to flower? What do you mean? Isn't one flower enough?"

Rosa's laugh was mischievous. "I AM a butterfly, and I need lots of flowers!"

Fred grabbed her, throwing her onto the bed. "I'll give you a bunch of flowers right now, you frivolous girl!" He playfully put his head into her pantyhose like a mugger. "Uh! Uh! This is a robbery, milady! Give me all your treasures now!"

Rosa played along, laughing. "Help me! Take all my treasures, but don't hurt me!"

Fred's voice was filled with playful malice. "I see your treasures, madam. They're magnificent!" He took the sock off, and they lost themselves in caresses, kisses, and the passionate dance that followed.

***

Back in the present, Rosa waved her hand in front of her face. "I'm not feeling well."

"Feeling sick?" Fred's concern was genuine.

"I'm… I'm short of breath. Let's go outside… It's very stuffy in here."

As they stood to leave, the café seemed to fade away, leaving only the echoes of their past and the unresolved tension of their present. They stepped into the cool air, the future uncertain, but the weight of their shared history ever present.

Rosa stood up abruptly, her chair scraping the floor with a screech that seemed to echo her internal turmoil. The café was bustling with activity, yet a bubble of isolation enveloped her. She needed air, space, a moment to clear her mind.

Fred, sensing the urgency, followed suit and addressed the concerned employee. "The lady is feeling unwell. We'll just step outside for a moment, and we'll be right back."

The terrace was a sanctuary amidst the chaos. They sat in silence, the weight of unspoken words pressing down on them. Fred broke the silence, his voice gentle. "Are you feeling better?"

Rosa nodded, a faint smile playing on her lips. "It's the baby moving. But I feel better now."

"How many months are you pregnant again?" Fred asked, his brow furrowing in concern.

"Seven months, Fred. I told you, "She replied, a hint of exasperation in her tone.

Fred sighed. "Right."

Rosa's eyes welled up with tears. "Alone… with a child coming into the world."

"Are you alone?" Fred's voice was barely a whisper, loaded with guilt.

"Of course! Since you left me," Rosa retorted, her words sharp.

Fred ran a hand through his hair, frustration etched on his face. "I didn't leave you. Things fell apart between us and the circumstances. There was a lack of communication, misunderstandings, resentments..."

Rosa interrupted, her voice rising. "And unmet expectations, which caused frustration and aggravated the arguments. What about your support? Zero!"

"There was interference too," Fred countered.

"What interference?" Rosa asked, genuinely perplexed.

"Interference from your friends… Martha, for example…"

Maria suddenly froze, and remembers the past conversations with Martha:

Martha and Rosa sat on a park bench, the sun casting long shadows. Martha's voice was fierce, cutting through the peaceful surroundings. "Holy shit, Rosa! I told you; you've got to get rid of that guy! That's why you're walking around like a zombie, whimpering!"

Rosa's voice trembled. "I don't know what to do…"

Martha's frustration was palpable. "Dating married guys—that's the worst! Do you spend weekends with him? No. And the vacations—Christmas, Easter—how do you spend them? Alone. And that's life? You're a spare biscuit to him!"

Rosa's eyes filled with tears. "But I love him… This is the only way to have it; that's how. Part-time."

Martha shook her head. "He and I get along well. There isn't enough time for misunderstandings or conflicts. But for him, you're just a hobby, like model airplanes. One day we'll be together for good…"

Martha's voice softened, yet remained firm. "Don't kid yourself, Rosa! Married men never leave their wives. You've got to give your life a direction; you can't stay there forever."

Rosa's voice cracked. "I don't know what to do…"

Martha's tone was fierce. " Kick him out! Show him the door! Reject him! You've got to start having a bit more self-esteem and stop being a heart doll in that guy's hands."

Rosa sobbed. "But I like him…"

Martha's expression softened, but her resolve remained. "I like a lot of things too. But there comes a time when we have to take our destiny into our own hands."

Rosa's revelation struck like a lightning bolt. "I'm pregnant… I bought the test at the pharmacy. The blue strip appeared."

Martha's eyes widened. "What?!"

Rosa nodded, tears streaming down her face. "I'm pregnant. I haven't spoken to him yet. We're taking a break…"

Back at the café, Rosa recited a poem with a melancholic smile.

"There is only one kind of beauty:

Yours.

Others say they are, but they lie, and they lie to them.

Yours shines

Yours feels, yours invades and ignites

Your beauty is dense and has the specific weight of intelligence

and the elegance of the dances.

Others say they have, but they lie, and they lie to them.

Yours is a beauty to look at.

Surrounded by lost mysteries

surrounded by distracted people

Looking for the place where you'll never be

Your beauty wasn't born; that's why it will never die.

It marks the hours, minutes, and seconds of those who deserve to wait.

They lie and lie to them.

There is only one kind of beauty: Yours"

Do you remember this poem? It was the first one you wrote for me."

Fred's eyes clouded with nostalgia. "Yes, I remember."

Rosa's voice wavered. "Do you still feel what you meant in the poem?"

Fred shook his head. "Those were different times. After that, the jealousy and blackmail started."

Rosa's eyes flashed with anger. "It wasn't jealousy, Fred… I was uncomfortable being a spare. When are we going to start making decisions instead of slaughtering each other?"

Fred's confusion was evident. "What decisions?"

Rosa took a deep breath. "Fred, my love… I'm pregnant…"

Fred's reaction was immediate. "So what?"

Rosa's voice trembled. "What do you want to do?"

Fred's face twisted in confusion. "What do I want to do? I don't understand."

Rosa's voice grew firmer. "Circumstances have changed."

Fred's eyes narrowed. "But… what are you talking about, Rosa? What's changed?"

Rosa's voice was steady. "I'm pregnant! It's your baby!"

Fred stared at her in disbelief. "But is this a cheap movie or what?"

Rosa's tone was calm but determined. "Yes, Fred. We're going to be the parents of a little girl!"

Fred's face turned pale. "Are you crazy? If I haven't been with you for months!"

Rosa's eyes were filled with a mix of hope and desperation. "You're wrong. It must have been six months since we decided to take a break. I'm seven and a half months pregnant."

Fred's voice was filled with frustration. "Is this a ploy to trap me? What are you thinking? Let's go back inside. Someone from work might see me."

Back at their table, the tension was palpable. Fred's head was in his hands. "I can't believe it! If it's true, why didn't you tell me sooner?"

Rosa's voice was soft but resolute. "I was just as surprised as you! For months, I didn't know what to do: raise her myself, make a mess… I didn't know what decision to make until it started to get late, and then I decided to go ahead and keep the girl."

Fred raised his head, his eyes searching Rosa's. "Oh my God! How… how are you going to deal with it?"

Rosa's voice was unwavering. "I'm sticking with it and raising the child. And the girl needs a father…"

Fred's voice was filled with disbelief. "What do you mean by that?"

Rosa's eyes locked onto Fred's. "You have to leave your wife, who doesn't bring you any happiness, and get together—me, you, and the little girl—in a happy family…"

Fred's voice was incredulous. "Are you nuts?"

Rosa's voice was filled with quiet determination. "But… you don't want me? Us?"

Fred's voice was weary. "I've told you a thousand times: It's not with the snap of a finger that I'm leaving a whole life behind. That would be unfair to my wife and children. I'm not old enough to start again from scratch or embark on adventures!"

Rosa's eyes were filled with tears. "So… you're going to abandon your daughter and me? I thought this pregnancy would change a little about your restrained and introverted manner, which is just a cover for your selfishness and self-indulgence. All you think about is your position in the company, surrounded by envious people."

Fred's voice was filled with resignation. "I did it for me, not because I was envious of others, but to get to the point where I don't feel envious of anyone."

***

The silence between them was thick, laden with the weight of unspoken truths and shattered dreams. Rosa's eyes burned with tears she refused to shed, her heart aching with the realization of the path she now had to walk alone. Fred's face was a mask of conflicted emotions, torn between duty and desire, the past and the present.

As they sat there, the world continued to move around them, indifferent to their personal tragedies. The café buzzed with life, conversations intermingling, creating a cacophony of normalcy that seemed almost mocking in its indifference.

Rosa took a deep breath, steeling herself for the future. She would raise her daughter with or without Fred's help. She would find strength in her love, in her hope, and in the small life growing inside her.

Fred looked at her one last time, his eyes filled with a mixture of regret and resignation. "I hope you find happiness, Rosa."

Rosa nodded; her voice steady. "I hope you find peace, Fred."

And with that, they parted ways, each stepping into an uncertain future, carrying the weight of their choices, their regrets, and their unresolved love.

Rosa sat in the dimly lit café, her heart pounding. The air felt thick with the weight of unspoken truths. Martha's words echoed in her mind; a haunting reminder of the reality she had tried so hard to ignore.

"Martha was right…" Rosa's voice was barely above a whisper, but it carried the weight of her resignation.

Fred's face contorted with anger. "FUCK THAT MARTHA! ALWAYS GETTING IN OUR WAY!"

Rosa shook her head slowly. "Martha… you may not like her… but she likes you even less. She knew that things would end up like this… that you would never exchange your life of facades, lies, and deceit for true love. I feel sorry for you."

Fred's frustration was palpable. "What do you want me to do? Leave everything and go to your single room house with another daughter?"

Rosa's voice trembled with sadness. "I see… you've made a very objective summary. If even an unborn child doesn't soften your heart, or the stone in its place… there's little more to be done or said. I loved you from day one. I had hopes and illusions and even dreams… but… a married man will always be a married man… everything else around him is just fun. To you, I was nothing more than an occasional restaurant, but the bill doesn't suit you now. You're going to run away, like you've done all your life… you're a coward!"

Fred tried to reason with her. "Rosa… you have to understand, if you were in my place, what would you do? I have a world that I've built up over the years… all the pieces are in place and stable… I'm not going to blow it up!"

Rosa's eyes filled with tears. "What do I do with the child?"

Fred pulled out his wallet. "I can help you with the medical expenses. I'll write you a check… I have said before."

Rosa's voice dripped with contempt. "You think I want a check… is that how you've been getting rid of mistresses: with a check?"

Fred hastily filled out a check and placed it on the table in front of her.

Rosa looks at the check, horrified "What is this?"

"No, Rosa! Stop being so dramatic! It's my way of assuming some of my responsibilities. I think it's enough for a private clinic and the rest."

Rosa's voice was hollow. "Who pays for her education?"

Fred looked away. "That's your responsibility… you're the one who decided to go ahead with the pregnancy."

Rosa, with a grimace of contempt and disgust, accepts the check.

Moments of silence enveloped them. Rosa stared at the check, then at Fred, then out of the café window. "And that's the end of it?"

Fred's voice was cold. "The end, how?"

Rosa's eyes filled with a mix of anger and sadness. "You don't even want to meet your daughter?"

Fred's voice wavered. "I don't know… I'll drop by sometime."

Rosa's heart shattered. "So… it's goodbye?"

Fred's voice was final. "Yes… goodbye."

Fred stood up and walked away. Rosa watched him leave, feeling a hollow ache in her chest. She picked up the check, slipped it into her purse, and stood up, heading for the exit. She was stopped by the employee.

"I'm sorry… please… the bill," the employee said politely.

Rosa looked at the table, then back at the employee, confusion washing over her. "… Yes… sorry. How much is it?"

"Six fifty," the employee replied.

Rosa searched her purse, found the money, and handed it to the employee. She left the café, her steps heavy with despair.

Outside, on the café terrace, Rosa paused, taking a deep breath. She walked to the parking lot, got into her car, and leaned over the steering wheel, a scream of frustration tearing from her throat. "FUCK!!"

She threw her bag into the back seat, glancing longingly at the façade of Fred's company before driving off through the city, tears streaming down her face.

The drive to her apartment was a blur. She parked, went inside, and dropped her handbag on the dining table. She took off her coat and shoes, the familiar presence of her cat offering a small comfort. She petted the cat, which jumped onto the table, then made her way to her room.

From a distance, the scene unfolded like a silent film. Rosa removed the fake pregnancy belly and hurled it against the wall, the thud echoing her internal anguish. She returned to the dining table, reached into her purse, and pulled out Fred's check. For a moment, she stared at it, the weight of her decisions pressing down on her.

With a resolve she hadn't felt in months, Rosa tore up the check, the pieces fluttering to the floor like broken promises. She sank into a chair, the cat curling up in her lap, and finally allowed herself to cry.

****

3.

SISTERS

The university loomed tall and imposing against the cerulean sky, its modern architecture stark yet elegant, a hub of youthful energy and academic rigor. Alice stepped out of the lecture hall; her mind still lost in the intricate web of theories her professor had unraveled. The sunlight was warm on her face, and she adjusted the strap of her backpack, taking in the familiar sight of students sprawled across the manicured lawns, laughing and chatting, as they soaked up the last of the afternoon sun.

As she walked towards the subway, the city pulsed around her—a living organism of steel and glass, humming with life. Alice moved through it with the practiced ease of someone who had long since mapped its rhythms, its cadences. The subway was crowded, the air thick with the scent of commuters and the distant screech of metal on metal. She found a seat near the window and watched as the world outside flickered past in a blur of motion—streets and buildings, trees and people—all merging into one continuous, unbroken stream.

Her thoughts, however, were elsewhere, floating back to the quietude of home, to the muted tones of her parents' house, where every object seemed to absorb sound rather than reflect it. The house was a sanctuary of sorts, though the atmosphere was often heavy, laden with unspoken worries and the weight of her father's frequent absences. As the subway emerged from the darkness of the tunnel into the late afternoon light, Alice felt a familiar pang of unease gnaw at the edges of her consciousness—something unamenable, but present, like a shadow in the corner of her vision.

By the time she arrived home, the sky had deepened to a dusky lavender. She pushed open the door and stepped inside, the familiar scent of her mother's cooking wafting through the air. But tonight, the house felt different—tense, expectant, as if holding its breath. Her mother was at the window, eyes red-rimmed and distant, while her father stood with his back to the room, a figure of stoic despair.

"Hello, Papa, hello Mama," Alice greeted, her voice cutting through the thick silence like a blade.

Her father turned slowly, his face hard with barely contained fury. "Where's your sister?"

Alice blinked, caught off guard by the sharpness in his tone. "Diana? She didn't come with me. I came straight from university... She must have gone back to her own place. We've never returned together. Why? What's happened?"

Her mother's voice trembled, a fragile thread of sound. "She was supposed to go to the dentist today, but they called to say she didn't show up for her appointment. And she's not answering her cell phone."

Alice felt her stomach drop, the unease she'd been carrying since the subway ride suddenly sharpening into something cold and real. "That's strange," she murmured, more to herself than to her parents. "She didn't mention any appointments..."

Her father's anger erupted like a storm. "My children have always been stupid! Irresponsible, without the slightest bit of sense in those empty heads!"

"Calm down, Diego," her mother interjected, her voice laced with exhaustion. "We won't get anywhere like this."

Alice stepped back, watching as the familiar scene unfolded—a dance of blame and frustration that had played out in countless variations over the years. "Try calling her again," her mother urged, turning to Alice with desperate eyes.

Alice fumbled for her phone, dialing Diana's number with fingers that suddenly felt clumsy and cold. The line rang and rang, each unanswered tone echoing the growing dread in her chest. "She's not picking up," she said finally, her voice barely above a whisper. "Her phone must be on silent."

"We've been trying since lunchtime," her mother replied, her hands wringing the edge of her apron. "Do you have the number of that boy— her friend?"

"I think so," Alice answered, scrolling through her contacts with a sense of urgency she couldn't quite suppress. She found the number and dialed, her heart pounding in her ears.

"Hello, Alice! what's up?" came the casual, slightly surprised voice of Di on the other end.

"Hi, Di!" she replied quickly. "Have you seen my sister today?"

There was a pause, and then, "Your sister? No, she didn't show up at the university today. She usually texts me if we're going to have lunch together... but nothing today."

Alice bit her lip. "Do you know where she might be?"

The boy's voice took on a teasing edge. "Whoa, your sister is very independent. I'm not the one to keep tabs on her, you know? She could be out partying for all I know."

Alice sighed, the flippant response doing nothing to ease her anxiety. "If you hear anything, please let me know. We haven't heard from her since this morning, and she missed an important appointment."

"Sure thing, Alice. I'll ask around, see if anyone's seen her."

Alice hung up and turned back to her parents, their anxious faces reflecting her own fear. "He hasn't seen her," she reported, her voice tight. "I'll call another friend."

But the calls yielded nothing—only more empty reassurances and promises to check in with others. With each dead end, the tension in the house grew thicker, until it felt like the very walls were closing in on them.

Her father slumped into a chair, burying his face in his hands. Her mother, eyes wide with panic, whispered, "What are we going to do? Why doesn't she show up?"

Alice, feeling the weight of their desperation pressing down on her, took a deep breath. "We need to call Emergency Services," she said, her voice firmer than she felt. "Dad, you should make the call."

But her father only shook his head, too overwhelmed to act. "I'm too nervous... Please, can you, do it?"

Alice nodded, though her hands trembled as she dialed the number. The voice on the other end was calm, almost detached, a stark contrast to the turmoil that churned within her.

"Good afternoon, what's the emergency?"

Alice swallowed hard. "Good afternoon. This is Alice Jacob. I need to report my sister missing."

The conversation that followed was a blur—questions and answers exchanged in a rhythm that felt unreal, disconnected from the fear that throbbed in her chest. When she finally hung up, she turned to her parents with a heavy heart. "We have to wait," she said, her voice barely audible. "If Diana doesn't show up in the meantime, we'll have to contact the police."

Her mother covered her face with her hands, her shoulders shaking with silent sobs. Her father stared at the floor, his expression one of helplessness and despair. And all Alice could do was sit with them, the three of them suspended in a liminal space, caught between hope and dread.

***

The day bled into night in a slow, inevitable descent. Outside, the sun dipped below the horizon, casting long shadows across the streets, while inside the house, time seemed to stretch and contract in strange, unpredictable ways. Hours passed in silence, broken only by the occasional murmur of reassurance, the soft sound of someone shifting in their seat, the creak of the floorboards as one of them moved restlessly from room to room.

By midnight, the house was shrouded in darkness, the only light coming from the dim glow of the kitchen, where Alice's father sat nursing a mug of hot milk. The air was thick with the scent of it, sweet and comforting, a stark contrast to the anxiety that hung over them like a shroud.

Alice, unable to sleep, padded softly into the kitchen, her bare feet cold against the tiles. Her father looked up as she entered, his eyes heavy with fatigue. "So, Dad... you can't sleep?" she asked, her voice a whisper in the stillness.

He shook his head, a tired smile tugging at the corners of his mouth. "I have trouble falling asleep," he admitted. "I thought some hot milk might help."

Alice nodded, sliding into the chair opposite him. "I sleep badly too," she confessed. "I always wake up startled."

For a moment, they sat in companionable silence, the kitchen a small island of light in the vast sea of night. Then, her father spoke again, his voice soft, almost tentative. "I've been wondering if I've been a good father to you."

Alice's heart clenched at the vulnerability in his words. "Of course you've been a good father," she replied, reaching out to touch his hand.

But he only sighed, a sound full of regret and self-doubt. "Because of my job as a truck driver, I'm not home much. I leave your mother alone with you both... A paternal presence is always needed in raising children."

"Don't worry," Alice reassured him, though her voice wavered. "We've managed very well."

But as she sat there, holding his hand, she couldn't help but wonder if he was right. If the absence of their father's steady, guiding hand had left them adrift, struggling to navigate the complexities of their lives without the anchor of his presence. And now, with Diana missing, that absence felt more acute than ever—a gaping hole in the fabric of their family, one that they could not easily mend.

The night stretched on, long and unforgiving, and as the hours slipped away, so too did their hope. They were left with nothing but the silence, the waiting, and the unspoken fear that Diana might never return

***

In the dim light of the kitchen, the sound of the kettle boiling filled the silence between them. The father, his shoulders hunched over the table, stared into his cup as if the answers he sought might be found in the steam rising from his tea. His face, etched with lines of worry and fatigue, betrayed the weight of his thoughts. Alice sat across from him, her posture rigid, reflecting the tension that had settled between them like a thick fog.

He broke the silence, his voice low, almost tentative, as if afraid of the answer. "I know I've been a bit harsh and rigid at times, Alice. But... I haven't been completely inflexible, have I?"

Alice looked up, her eyes meeting his. There was a softness in her gaze, a daughter's compassion for a father who had always tried his best, even when his best felt like too much. "I have nothing to complain about, Dad."

The father nodded, but the uncertainty lingered in his expression, like a shadow that refused to lift. "Your sister, though... she's so rebellious, always has her head in the clouds. It's hard not to be concerned. Your mother tells me these are just phases, that adolescence is difficult... but what if it's more than that?"

Alice's gaze softened further, her tone gentle but firm. "Diana has her own personality, Dad. She doesn't bother anyone. She's just… finding her way."

A silence followed, heavy with unspoken fears. The father leaned back in his chair, his brow furrowed in thought. "But she chooses her friends so badly. That Di guy, for example… He's trouble, Alice. I've heard things… bad things."

Alice sighed, the weight of her father's words pressing down on her. "Di has his quirks, yes, but he's not a bad person. He's just… different."

"Different?" Her father's voice rose, his frustration seeping through. "I've heard he was caught sneaking into people's yards, letting their dogs loose! That's not just different, Alice—that's trouble."

Alice shook her head, trying to deflect the intensity of his worry. "That's just kids' stuff, Dad. It doesn't mean he's a bad influence on Diana."

The father's voice grew quieter, tinged with a desperation that Alice rarely heard from him. "I don't trust him, Alice. If anything happens to Diana, I'll never forgive myself. I've been too hard on her… or maybe not hard enough."

Alice reached across the table, her hand resting on his. "Nothing's happened to Diana, Dad. She's always been impulsive, but she's not reckless. She's probably just staying at a friend's place."

He looked at her, his eyes weary and filled with doubt. "The problem is, there are friends… and there are friends. I don't know who she's with, and that scares me."

Alice squeezed his hand gently before standing up. "Don't worry, Dad. Everything will be fine. Try to get some rest. Tomorrow is a new day."

The father nodded, though his gaze remained fixed on the table. "Five more minutes… and then I'll try to sleep."

***

Morning crept into the house like an unwelcome guest, its light seeping through the curtains and casting long shadows on the walls. The father was already up, his eyes red-rimmed from lack of sleep, the television murmuring softly in the background. Alice entered the room, offering a weary smile as she kissed him on the cheek. "Good morning, Dad. How are you feeling?"

He sighed, rubbing a hand across his face. "I slept for maybe an hour. I'm exhausted, Alice. But I can't stop thinking… horrible thoughts keep running through my head. I just want to make them stop."

Alice sat down beside him, her hand resting on his arm. "In times like these, sleep feels like a luxury. But we have to trust that everything will work out. We have to believe that Diana is okay, wherever she is."

The father's expression darkened. "It's hard to believe that when all I can do is blame myself. We've always had a difficult relationship, and now… now she's gone. Adolescence… it's supposed to be a time of discovery, but all it feels like is disobedience and confrontation."

Alice shook her head, her voice soft but insistent. "It's part of growing up, Dad. Finding your place in the world means testing boundaries, even if it means clashing with the people you love."

The father leaned forward, his voice rising with emotion. "But I didn't have those problems with you, Alice. You've always been so peaceful, so compliant."

"We're not all the same, Dad. Sometimes it's easier not to clash… but that doesn't mean Diana is wrong for being different."

His frustration boiled over, his voice sharp and brittle. "If something happens to her, I'll never forgive myself! I should have done more… or maybe less… I don't know."

From the kitchen, the mother's voice drifted in, calm but firm. "Sometimes you're too authoritarian, Diego."

He whipped his head around, his voice cutting through the air like a knife. "Shut up! You don't know anything! Don't bother me!"

Alice placed a soothing hand on his shoulder. "Dad… we can't undo the past. What's done is done. But we can call the police, report her missing… 24 hours have already passed."

The father nodded, his anger giving way to a weary resignation. "Yes… yes, you're right."

Alice pulled out her phone, her fingers trembling slightly as she dialed the number. The voice on the other end was calm, methodical, as she explained the situation, provided the details they needed. When she hung up, she turned to her father, her expression resolute.

"They're sending detectives over to the house. They'll help us find her, Dad. We just have to hold on a little longer."

***

The doorbell rang, its sound cutting through the tense quiet that had settled over the house. Alice's mother opened the door to reveal two detectives, their faces stern but compassionate as they introduced themselves. Detective Sheila Son and her colleague stepped inside, their presence a reminder that the situation was now out of their hands, that professionals were taking over.

The detectives asked their questions, their voices calm and measured, as they gathered the details of Diana's disappearance. Alice answered as best she could, though each response felt like a small admission of defeat, a reminder of how little she knew about her sister's life.

"No," she said when asked if Diana had ever disappeared before. "This is the first time anything like this has happened."

Detective Son nodded, her expression thoughtful. "And her phone is still on, you say?"

Alice nodded, a small flicker of hope igniting in her chest. "Yes. It rings, but she doesn't answer."

The detective offered a small, reassuring smile. "That's a good sign. It means she might be somewhere safe, just not ready to talk yet."

But the hope was short-lived, extinguished by the father's next words. "She's been hanging out with this guy, Di. I don't trust him. He's older, covered in tattoos… I wouldn't be surprised if he's involved in something illegal."

Alice bristled at her father's assumption, her voice rising in defense of her sister's friend. "Dad, that's not fair. Di's not a bad person just because he looks different. Tattoos don't make you a criminal."

But the father shook his head, his expression set in stone. "You can't see it, Alice. We're lowering our standards, accepting things that shouldn't be acceptable."

Detective Son interjected, her voice patient but firm. "We'll look into it, sir. For now, let's focus on finding Diana."

As the detectives continued their questioning, Alice felt the weight of her father's fear pressing down on her, the burden of his guilt, his regret. But beneath it all, there was a quiet determination in her heart— a resolve to find her sister, to bring her home, and to prove that sometimes, different didn't mean dangerous.

"Can we go inside?" Can we come in?" Asked Sheila with a certain authority in her voice.

Everyone went into the living room.

The room was a blend of tension and exhaustion. Sheila, the lead detective, leaned back in one chair, her eyes sharp as they followed Alice's every move. The daylight filtering through the window cast long shadows across the floor, adding to the weight of the situation. Alice held her phone in trembling hands, her fingers scrolling through the contacts until she found the name she was looking for. "Has anyone contacted this guy Di? Sheila asked.

"Yes, I spoke to him," Alice said, her voice steady despite the anxiety gnawing at her insides. "He said he hadn't seen Diana for about three days."

Sheila nodded, her expression unreadable. "Can you give me his cell phone number? We need to talk to him directly."

Alice quickly found the number, holding out her phone for Sheila to see. The detective scribbled the digits into her notebook with practiced efficiency, her pen moving in swift, confident strokes.

"Does Diana study?" Sheila asked, shifting the conversation back to routine inquiries.

"Yes," Alice's father interjected, his voice gruff with the remnants of sleep and worry. "She started university this year."

Sheila's gaze flicked back to Alice, searching for more details. "And what's her normal route to get to university?"

Alice hesitated, picturing the familiar paths her sister took each day. "We have a bus stop right outside our door. Sometimes she takes the Metro, though that requires walking down a small avenue to the station."

"Is it a quiet avenue?" Sheila's question was laced with concern, the subtle implication of danger lingering in the air.

Alice shook her head. "No, it's usually busy, lots of movement."

Sheila took note, her pen scratching across the paper. "And when she takes the bus, does she get off right at the university building?"

"Yes," Alice confirmed. "It's door-to-door."

Sheila's questions continued, peeling back the layers of Diana's routine, her habits, her friends. "What does she do in her spare time?"

The father let out a frustrated sigh. "That's what I'd like to know!"

Alice ignored the jab, focusing on the detective. "She usually has lunch in the canteen or at a nearby McDonald's. After classes, she often studies with friends at a library in the city center."

"And on weekends?" Sheila pressed, her questions methodical.

"Saturday afternoons, she always goes to the Sports Pavilion to practice fencing. She loves it," Alice said, her voice softening at the memory of her sister, poised with a sword in hand, her face lit up with concentration and joy.

Sheila's pen paused. "The coach… is it a man or a woman?"

"I think it's a man," Alice replied, trying to recall the few details Diana had shared.

"Hmm…" Sheila hummed thoughtfully, jotting down the information. "Do you have any photos of Diana that I could use?"

Alice's mother, silent until now, retrieved a photo from the side table. The image showed Diana with her wide smile, her eyes bright with life. Sheila took a quick snapshot with her phone, offering a small nod of thanks. "Let's hope Diana turns up soon."

With that, Sheila and her colleague left the house, the atmosphere heavy with unsaid fears and unspoken hopes.

***

Outside, the sun had dipped lower in the sky, casting the neighborhood in a warm, golden glow. Sheila stepped onto the porch, her phone already in hand as she dialed the number Alice had provided. The phone rang twice before a voice answered.

"Hello?"

"Good afternoon," Sheila began, her tone professional but firm. "This is Sheila, a police detective. We need your help regarding the disappearance of Diana Jacob."

There was a pause on the other end before the voice responded, tinged with surprise. "What? She hasn't shown up yet?"

"I'm afraid not," Sheila confirmed. "Would it be too much trouble for you to come to the station as soon as possible?"

"No problem," the voice replied, now filled with urgency. "I'll be there in fifteen minutes."

"Ask for Detective Sheila when you arrive," she instructed, her voice steady.

"Okidoki! See you soon!" The call ended, and Sheila pocketed her phone, her mind already shifting to the next steps.

Out of the corner of her eye, Sheila noticed a figure approaching—uninvited and unwelcome. A journalist, camera in hand, with the look of someone hungry for a story.

"Oh, no," her colleague muttered under his breath. "You're like morticians—you appear out of nowhere."

"Good afternoon to you too," the journalist replied with a smirk, unfazed by the hostility.

Sheila crossed her arms, unimpressed. "What are you doing here? Isn't there blood elsewhere?"

The journalist shrugged; his tone casual. "I heard about the disappearance of a girl…"

"And how did you know?" Sheila's colleague challenged; his voice tinged with suspicion.

"I have my sources," the journalist replied, his grin widening.

"Your sources must be the police radio, I bet," the colleague shot back, his eyes narrowing.

"I neither confirm nor deny," the journalist said, unbothered.

"You know it's illegal to hack into police radio frequencies?" The warning was clear, but the journalist remained undeterred.

"We're in a bad mood today," the journalist remarked, still smiling. "All I need is a photo for the evening news. Spreading the word usually helps the police."

"Damn vultures," Sheila's colleague muttered, but Sheila held up a hand, signaling him to stop.

"She's partly right," Sheila conceded, pulling out her phone. "What's your number?"

"835-556623," the journalist replied, his tone almost cheerful.

Sheila sent the photo quickly, her mind already moving on to the next task as the journalist thanked her with a wry comment about "female solidarity."

As they headed to their car, Sheila's mind raced, the case unfolding in layers she was only beginning to see. They drove in silence, the weight of their responsibility pressing down on them as they made their way back to the station.

***

The police station was a hive of activity, officers moving with purpose, phones ringing, and the low murmur of conversations filling the air. Sheila and her colleague occupied two desks separated by a few meters, their computers open as they reviewed the information they'd gathered so far. Sheila was focused, her mind sharp as she pieced together the puzzle of Diana's disappearance.

Her colleague offered her a piece of gum, but Sheila declined, too immersed in her thoughts. She was interrupted by the receptionist's voice calling her name.

"Detective Sheila, there's someone here to see you."

Sheila glanced up, spotting a young man standing at the counter. He was tall, with a scruffy appearance, but there was a nervous energy about him. She approached him with measured steps.

"Yes?" she asked, her voice neutral.

"Are you Detective Sheila?" the young man asked, his voice uncertain.

"Yes…" Sheila responded, her gaze narrowing slightly.

"My name is Dimur… but I guess you wanted to talk to me?" he said, shifting uncomfortably under her scrutiny.

"Dimur?" Sheila's eyes flickered with recognition. "Ah, Di! Come in."

She led him to her desk, gesturing for him to sit down. Her colleague joined them, taking a seat nearby, his presence a silent reminder of the seriousness of the situation.

"Thank you for coming," Sheila began, her tone professional. "We'd like to know a bit more about your relationship with Diana."

Dimur fidgeted, clearly uneasy, but nodded in agreement. "Sure."

"When was the last time you saw Diana?" Sheila asked, her eyes locked on his.

Dimur hesitated, his mind searching for the memory. "I don't know… two or three days ago, in the university garden."

"Are you also studying at university?" Sheila pressed, watching his reaction closely.

Dimur shook his head. "No. I'm… well… I'm unemployed right now."

"Unemployed?" Sheila's voice held a note of skepticism. "And where do you get the money for drugs?"

Dimur's eyes widened in shock, his gaze snapping to Sheila. "Drugs? I don't know anything about that!"

Sheila didn't flinch, her expression unreadable. "No? Not even a joint once in a while? So, what are you doing chasing university girls? Is it to talk philosophy?"

Dimur's face flushed with a mix of confusion and indignation. "I meet all kinds of people: students, store assistants, truck drivers, hairdressers."

"A popular boy, then!" Sheila's tone was dry, almost mocking. "How old are you?"

"Twenty-five," Dimur replied, his voice steadying.

"Don't you think you're too old to be dating a seventeen-year-old girl like Diana?" Sheila's question was sharp, cutting through the tension.

"I don't hang out with her," Dimur insisted, his voice rising. "I only know her through mutual friends! But… am I being accused of something?"

"Not yet," Sheila replied calmly. "We just want to find Diana. Then… we'll see."

She leaned forward slightly, her gaze piercing. "The last time you 'hung out' with Diana, did you notice anything unusual about her? Was she happy, sad? Did you smoke a joint?"

Dimur groaned, exasperated. "There you go again! I told you, I'm not into that!"

"Okay," Sheila conceded, her tone softening just a fraction. "What do you think about Diana being missing??"

Dimur swallowed hard, his throat bobbing. He seemed to realize he was being cornered, like a rat in a maze with no exit.

Sheila nodded slowly, as if considering his words, though her eyes never left his face. "Okay. But what did you think of her that day? Did she make any unusual comments?"

Dimur hesitated, his brow furrowed in thought. "That day... I don't remember anything special; she talks a lot about her problems with her father. He seems to be quite authoritarian..."

"Problems with her father," Sheila mused, tapping her pen on the desk thoughtfully. "But do you have any idea where she is? Is she at a friend's house? Has she run away from home? Did she have enemies?"

"I have no idea," Dimur said, shaking his head. "Have you asked the family?"

Sheila's expression hardened, the calm façade cracking ever so slightly. "Of course we asked, you idiot! What do you think we're doing here: polishing badges all day?"

Dimur flinched at her sharp tone, shrinking into himself. "Sorry," he muttered, his voice barely above a whisper.

"Speaking of family," Sheila continued, her voice softening just a fraction, "do you get on well with Diana's family?"

Dimur hesitated, glancing nervously at Sheila's colleague, who had been watching the exchange in silence. "I picked Alice up there once in a while... nothing special."

Sheila's eyes narrowed as she exchanged a glance with her colleague. "But then... you're going out with Alice too?"

Dimur's face flushed, and he stammered, "I wanted to say: Diana." His words fumbled over each other, the slip of the tongue betraying more than he intended. "Can I go?" he asked, desperation creeping into his voice.

Sheila studied him for a long moment, then reached into her pocket and pulled out a business card, holding it out to him. "When you know anything that will help us locate Diana, let us know, okay?"

Dimur nodded hastily, snatching the card from her hand. "Yes, of course," he said, his voice shaky as he bolted from the room.

As the door clicked shut behind him, Sheila's colleague finally spoke. "The boy knows something, don't you think?"

Sheila leaned back in her chair, her expression contemplative. "Yes," she said slowly, "to put it mildly—I said a lot. There's some kind of scam going on here."

The colleague shrugged, reaching for a packet of chewing gum on his desk. "I'm not sure, but it sounds more like a case of a rebellious girl running away from home to teach her parents a lesson."

Sheila shot him a wry smile. "You've solved the case, then?"

"Obviously!" he retorted, popping a piece of gum into his mouth. "No one can stop this brain when I turn it on full speed!"

Sheila chuckled, the tension in the room easing slightly. "You're in this department, not because of your intelligence, but because you're good at licking boots while you tighten their laces!"

Her colleague burst into laughter, his hearty chuckle filling the small office. "And you," he countered, "are in that position because they needed to fulfill their woman quota!"

"Right," Sheila shot back, grinning, "and you're here to fill the gorilla quota!"

Their laughter was interrupted by the shrill ring of the phone on the desk. The colleague answered, his tone shifting to one of professionalism. "Yes? Good afternoon, Chief! I'll put Detective Sheila on." He handed the receiver to Sheila, his expression serious now.

"Ah! Good afternoon, boss!" Sheila said, her voice tinged with a mixture of respect and apprehension. "Yes... Hum, hum. Well... we're following up; we've already been to the family, and we've just taken statements from the girl's best friend..." She listened intently, her expression unreadable. "Yes, of course! All the agents are on alert, with instructions to locate her. It looks like it's a case of a rebellious girl who wants to teach her parents a lesson. Thank you! Good afternoon, Chief!" She handed the phone back to her colleague with a sigh.

"We've got the boss on our ass," she muttered, rubbing her temples.

Her colleague shrugged, leaning back in his chair. "It's a small, quiet town, and the slightest thing sets the alarm bells ringing."

"Anyway!" Sheila said, standing up and stretching. "It's a small town, but she could be a long way from here! She could even be in Paris for all we know."

Her colleague chuckled again, his mood lightening. "Everything will be fine. Let's get something to eat—I had a poor lunch today."

Together, they left the office, the weight of the missing girl still lingering in the air like a shadow.

***

The next day dawned with a heavy sky, the clouds thick and low, threatening rain. Alice stood at the bus stop, leaning against the cold concrete wall, her eyes glued to the screen of her cell phone. Her fingers moved with a practiced ease, scrolling through messages, her mind elsewhere. To her right, a display of household appliances flickered behind the glass of a shop window, a row of televisions tuned to the news. The sound was muted, but the images on the screens were enough to catch her attention.

A photo appeared on all the screens at once, a familiar face with the word "MISSING" emblazoned beneath it. Alice's breath caught in her throat as she realized she was staring at an image of herself. Panic surged through her, and she quickly averted her gaze, her heart pounding in her chest.

The bus arrived with a screech of brakes, and Alice hurriedly boarded, her mind racing. She found a seat near the back, her hands trembling as she clutched her phone. She could feel eyes on her, the weight of scrutiny pressing down, but she kept her gaze fixed on the floor, willing the ride to pass quickly.

The bus rumbled through the streets, finally arriving at the shopping center. Alice stepped off and made her way inside, her movements quick, almost furtive. The familiar bustle of the mall surrounded her, a cacophony of voices and footsteps, but it did little to ease the unease gnawing at her insides. She headed for the elevator, her destination clear in her mind: the restaurant area, a place where she could blend in, disappear among the crowd.

As the elevator doors slid open, Alice stepped out and moved towards one of the fast-food counters. She placed her order mechanically, barely registering the cashier's cheerful greeting. With her tray in hand, she found a secluded table near the edge of the dining area and sat down, her phone once again occupying her full attention.

But she wasn't alone. Unbeknownst to her, two security guards were watching her from a distance. The first guard, a stocky man with a shaved head, spoke into his walkie-talkie, his eyes never leaving Alice. "Where are you? On the first floor? Get up here to the restaurant. Run!"

A few minutes passed, and the second guard, a younger man with a thin mustache, joined his colleague. "What's up, bro?" he asked, following the older man's gaze.

"See that girl alone on her cell phone?" The first guard's voice was low, almost a whisper.

The second guard squinted, scanning the tables. "Which girl? Where?"

"There," the first guard said, nodding towards Alice. "Next to that couple with the kids."

The younger guard's eyes widened as he finally spotted her. "The red-haired girl?" he asked, though his tone suggested he already knew the answer.

"That's right," the first guard confirmed. "Doesn't that look like the girl on the news who's reported missing?"

The second guard stared for a moment longer, then nodded slowly. "It really does look like her! What are we going to do?"

The first guard switched the frequency on his walkie-talkie, his voice urgent as he spoke into it. "Switch to frequency 81 and call the police. I'll talk to her. You get close, but don't join me, okay?"

"Right," the second guard agreed, his face set in determination.

As the younger guard stepped back, the older one approached Alice's table, a practiced smile on his face. "Good afternoon!" he said, his tone friendly but firm. "Sorry to bother you... but you don't usually come to this center, do you?"

Alice looked up, her eyes wary. "Huh? I came here to make some photocopies," she replied, her voice guarded.

The guard nodded, as if considering her words. "Yeah... the good thing about shopping centers is that you can make photocopies whenever you want."

Alice frowned, suspicion creeping into her expression. "I think so, it's an advantage."

The guard smiled again, trying to keep the conversation light. "Soon, a large candy and chocolate store will open on the second floor. I assume you like sweets..."

Alice's eyes narrowed, her suspicion deepening. "I like it. Like almost everyone, I guess."

The second guard had moved closer now, just within earshot. He nodded slightly to his colleague, confirming that the call had been made.

The first guard's smile faltered slightly as he took a deep breath. "May I ask your name?"

Alice stiffened, her eyes darting between the two men. "My name? Why do you want to know my name? What's going on here? I don't like your behavior! I'm leaving!" She pushed her chair back, preparing to bolt.

The first guard raised his hands placatingly, stepping back slightly. "I beg your pardon. Don't leave—there are some people who would like to talk to you. Just a minute..."

But Alice was already on her feet, her face flushed with anger and fear. "BUT WHAT'S GOING ON? LET ME GO, OR I'LL CALL SECURITY GUARD!" she shouted, her voice rising.

"We're Security Guards," the first man said quickly, his tone urgent but calm. "Don't worry, it'll only take a few minutes. I apologize once again. Let's wait, please..."

Alice hesitated, her breath coming in short, quick bursts as she assessed the situation. She was trapped, but she wasn't about to go down without a fight. As the seconds ticked by, the tension between them crackled like electricity, the calm before the storm.

***

Alice sat quietly at the metal table, the harsh fluorescent light above casting an unforgiving glow on the room. The sterile smell of the police station filled her nostrils as she adjusted her position, trying to find comfort on the hard plastic chair. Detective Sheila Son and her colleague had just arrived, their presence commanding the small space.

"Good afternoon, everyone," Sheila greeted, her tone professional but edged with authority. Her sharp eyes scanned the room before landing on Alice. She took a step forward, her gaze shifting from the girl to a photograph on her cell phone. "Is this the girl you were looking for?" one of the security guards asked, nodding towards Alice.

Sheila didn't respond immediately, instead comparing the photo on her phone with the girl sitting before her. "So, Diana," she finally said, a slight smirk tugging at the corner of her lips. "You finally decided to show up?"

Alice's eyes widened in surprise. "Detective Sheila, my name is not Diana!" she protested, her voice steady but laced with confusion.

The second security guard, who had been observing quietly until now, chuckled with a hint of sarcasm. "And my name is Mariella!" he quipped, clearly enjoying the moment.

Alice shook her head, frustration bubbling up inside her. "But… it's a mistake!" she insisted, her voice rising.

Sheila, seemingly unfazed by Alice's protests, pulled out her cell phone. "I will notify the family that the girl has been located," she said, dialing a number. But just as she pressed the call button, a sudden, shrill ring echoed through the room, coming from Alice's pocket.

Sheila froze, her eyes narrowing in confusion as she watched Alice pull out her phone. "Detective," Alice said slowly, holding up her ringing phone, "why are you calling me?"

Sheila stared at the girl, her brow furrowing in disbelief. "But… I'm calling Alice Jacob!" she said, her voice tinged with bewilderment.

"I'm Alice Jacob, Detective," Alice replied, the confusion now mirrored in her own expression.

"What do you mean?" Sheila's voice faltered slightly, her confident demeanor cracking. "But you look just like the picture they gave me!"

Alice took a deep breath, her patience wearing thin. "Because I'm Diana's twin sister," she explained, her tone calm but firm.

The room fell silent as Sheila processed this information. "Twin sister?" she echoed, the realization dawning on her. "What's going on here? I'm confused!"

Alice met Sheila's gaze, her expression steady. "The photo you have is of my sister, Diana. We look alike, but I'm Alice."

Sheila rubbed her temples, a headache threatening to form. "Well… this is getting to be a real mess," she muttered under her breath. She looked up at Alice, her expression serious. "Alice, you're coming with us to the police station."

Alice blinked, her confusion deepening. "But to the police station, for what purpose?" she asked, her voice tinged with both curiosity and apprehension.

Sheila turned to the security guards, nodding in acknowledgment. "Thank you for your cooperation," she said, her tone professional once more. "You are good professionals."

The first security guard smiled, a touch of pride in his demeanor. "Well… that's what we're here for! I hope you find the girl," he said before both guards withdrew from the room, leaving Alice alone with the detectives.

Sheila turned back to Alice, her gaze firm. "You're coming with me to the police station," she repeated, her tone leaving no room for argument.

Alice swallowed hard, trying to keep her composure. "But why?" she asked, her voice small in the echoing room.

Sheila's colleague, who had remained silent until now, let out a low chuckle. "The girl thinks she's in a movie and that she's entitled to a phone call," he murmured, clearly amused.

Ignoring her colleague, Sheila softened her tone slightly. "You're not under arrest, Alice," she assured her. "I have questions to ask you when you're not with your parents."

Alice hesitated, weighing her options. "Can I make a phone call?" she asked, her voice trembling slightly.

"Of course, you can call," Sheila replied, nodding. "You're not under arrest."

Alice made the call, her hands shaking slightly as she dialed the familiar number. As she spoke quietly into the phone, Sheila and her colleague exchanged glances, their expressions unreadable.

A short while later, they arrived at the police station. The small, sterile interrogation room felt even more oppressive than the previous room. Alice sat at the table, her posture tense as Sheila and her colleague took their seats across from her.

"Honestly… I think this is unnecessary," Alice said, her voice steady despite the situation.

Sheila leaned forward, her gaze piercing. "Everything is necessary when it comes to finding your sister," she said, her tone serious. "What are you hiding?"

Alice's eyes widened in shock. "We're not hiding anything!" she exclaimed, frustration seeping into her voice. "Now I'm to blame for my sister's disappearance? Instead of bothering me here, you should be out there looking for her—instead of sitting here, at your desk, watching the case unfold under your nose!"

Sheila's expression softened slightly, though her gaze remained sharp. "Well… we weren't the ones who forgot to inform us that Diana had a twin sister," she said, a hint of reproach in her tone. "Don't you think we should have been told? I suspected something when I saw the photo your mother gave me… you look a lot like her, or she like you… whatever."

Alice sighed, the tension in her shoulders easing just a fraction. "Yes, we're alike," she admitted, her voice resigned.

Sheila's gaze intensified as she leaned closer. "I'm going to ask you very directly: do you know where your sister is?"

Alice met her gaze, her expression defiant. "I don't know! Diana has her life, and I have mine!" she retorted, her voice firm.

Sheila didn't back down. "But do you know where your sister is, or not?" she pressed. "Diana could be in danger. You need to be open and honest with us, Alice. I know that when we're young, we sometimes make mistakes, but there's no point in trying to escape from the mistakes we make. Every day we have people in this police station who have made mistakes and don't want to face up to them."

Before Alice could respond, the door burst open, and another officer entered the room, a sense of urgency in his movements. "Detective Sheila," he said quickly, his voice laced with concern. "We've got a lead on Diana."

Sheila's eyes widened, a mix of relief and tension flooding her expression. She glanced back at Alice, her expression softening slightly. "We'll continue this conversation later," she said before rising from her seat.

As Sheila and her colleague hurried out of the room, Alice was left alone, her mind racing. The walls of the interrogation room seemed to close in on her, the weight of her sister's disappearance pressing down like a heavy, invisible force.

Sheila might have found a lead, but for Alice, the mystery was far from over.

***

The Jacob's living room was silent, the air thick with tension. Sheila stood at the center, her eyes locked on Mr. Diego, a man whose rigid posture and clenched jaw betrayed the storm brewing within him. The walls of the room seemed to close in around them, the gravity of the conversation pressing down on everyone present. Diana sat in the corner, her gaze fixed on the floor, her shoulders hunched as if trying to make herself as small as possible.

Mr. Diego: you have to accept your daughter Diana's differences. She didn't choose to be like this. As much as it costs her, her daughter has a relationship with another girl. One phone call was all it took to find her at her friend's house. I spoke to Diana and your reactions when you found out about the affair, made her leave the house because her safety could be at stake.

"But I would never hurt my daughters!" shouted a cornered Diego.

Sheila took a deep breath, her voice steady and measured as she began to speak. "Tolerating difference is not just an act of kindness," she said, her words carefully chosen, "but a recognition that all human beings have the right to love and be loved, to live their authentic lives, and to be who they truly are, without fear of persecution or marginalization."

Her voice resonated with a quiet strength, each word carrying the weight of years of experience and understanding. "Every person, regardless of their sexual orientation, deserves to live in a world where freedom and equality are non-negotiable values," she continued, her gaze unwavering as she addressed Mr. Diego directly. "Mr. Diego, you are still a young man; you should understand the times better."

Mr. Diego shifted uncomfortably in his chair, his eyes flickering between Sheila and the daughter he barely recognized anymore. His hands trembled slightly, the tension in the room palpable. But Sheila pressed on, her voice growing firmer, more insistent.

"True tolerance goes beyond simply accepting the existence of others," she said, her tone leaving no room for argument. "It requires us to celebrate diversity, to learn from each other, and to build a society where all voices are heard and respected. It demands that we question our own prejudices, that we educate the next generations about the importance of inclusion, and that we continually strive to create environments where everyone can thrive."

Diana's father looked down at his hands, his mind struggling to absorb the magnitude of Sheila's words. His life had been built on traditions, on a belief in certain immutable truths. But now, those truths were being challenged in ways he had never anticipated.

"Do you understand, Mr. Diego?" Sheila asked, her voice softening slightly as she sensed the turmoil within him. "We must remember that homosexuality is not a choice, but a natural expression of human diversity. And as such, it deserves to be treated with the same respect and dignity as any other form of love and identity."

Mr. Diego's breath caught in his throat, his heart pounding in his chest as he grappled with the implications of Sheila's words. He had always thought of himself as a man of principle, someone who knew right from wrong. But now, confronted with the reality of his daughter's life, he felt the ground shifting beneath his feet, his certainties crumbling like sand.

"Every time we choose tolerance," Sheila continued, her voice now tinged with a quiet intensity, "we are one step closer to a world where humanity is defined by its capacity to love, and not by its differences."

The room was still, the only sound the faint hum of the air conditioning. Mr. Diego's eyes met Sheila's, and for a moment, something passed between them—an unspoken understanding, a recognition of shared humanity.

"Today, by committing ourselves to tolerance," Sheila said, her voice almost a whisper, "we are actually committing ourselves to a fairer, more equitable, and more loving future. We are choosing to build bridges instead of barriers, to choose understanding over judgment, and to celebrate the richness that diversity brings to our lives."

Mr. Diego's gaze shifted to his daughter, who still sat quietly in the corner, her head bowed. A lump formed in his throat as he took in the sight of her—the same girl he had raised, the same girl he had loved, and yet somehow, she seemed so different now, so distant.

"Do you understand, Mr. Diego?" Sheila asked, her tone gentle but insistent. "We must accept our children as they are. Neither you nor anyone else will be able to change Diana. Do we understand?"

Mr. Diego's voice was barely audible as he responded, his words thick with emotion. "As long as they're kissing away from me…" he muttered, his eyes still fixed on the floor.

Sheila nodded slowly, her expression one of quiet resolve. "That's it: you've made a commitment," she said, her voice firm. "And now I'm talking as a police officer: I'm going to open a parental monitoring procedure."

Mr. Diego looked up sharply, his eyes wide with alarm. "But I never hurt my daughter!" he protested, his voice rising in desperation.

Sheila met his gaze steadily, her tone unwavering. "But she ran away from home," she said simply. "We're obliged to open this follow-up process. Once a month, a social worker will come to visit, to see how things are going. I'm sorry, but I have to. Right now, it would be good for my soul to see Father and Daughter reconciled."

For a long moment, the room was silent, the weight of Sheila's words hanging in the air. Then, slowly, Diana stood up, her movements tentative and uncertain. She took a few hesitant steps toward her father, her eyes glistening with unshed tears.

Mr. Diego looked at his daughter, his heart aching with a mixture of love, regret, and confusion. And then, as if drawn by some invisible force, he opened his arms, and Diana stepped into his embrace, her body trembling as she held on to him.

Sheila watched the scene unfold, a faint smile tugging at the corners of her lips. She knew that this was just the beginning, that the road ahead would be long and difficult for both father and daughter. But for now, in this moment, there was a glimmer of hope—a chance for healing, for understanding, for reconciliation.

As Diana and her father held each other, Sheila and her colleague quietly slipped out of the room, leaving the family to their private moment. Outside, the sun was beginning to set, casting a warm, golden light over the city.

Sheila took a deep breath, the cool evening air filling her lungs as she walked toward the police car parked at the curb. Her colleague fell into step beside her, his expression thoughtful.

"Nice speech you gave to the girl's father," he remarked, his tone admiring.

Sheila smiled faintly; her eyes distant as she reflected on the conversation. "I already know this speech by heart," she replied, her voice tinged with a hint of weariness. "All my life, I've also been the victim of discrimination from people like Mr. Diego."

Her colleague nodded in understanding; his gaze fixed on the horizon as they approached the car. "They'll be okay," he said quietly, more a statement of hope than certainty.

Sheila didn't respond, but as they climbed into the car and pulled away from the curb, she allowed herself a moment of quiet satisfaction. The road ahead might be uncertain, but for now, she had done what she could. And sometimes, that was enough.

As the car drove through the city streets, the fading light casting long shadows across the pavement, Sheila felt a sense of peace settle over her—a peace that came not from the certainty of the future, but from the knowledge that, today, she had chosen to stand on the side of love, of understanding, of tolerance.

And in a world that so often seemed divided by fear and prejudice, that choice felt like a victory.

****